Foreword

Douglas Lister has served the Church, its Lord and its people with a combination of courage and distinction. His career shows something of the enormous variety of experience which ministry in the Church of Scotland can offer to a person who is spurred more by the needs of those charged to his care than by ecclesiastical advancement.

For me, the highlights of Douglas Lister's ministry were his service in Germany, in Egypt and in his Largo Parish in Fife. His time as a chaplain in post-war Germany reads more like an Ian Fleming spy story than a record of the predictable routines of a minister of religion. I'm tempted to re-tell the more exciting tales which have sprung from each of these places, but that would be impermissible in a foreword. My only recourse is to urge you to skip the foreword and read "The Luneburg Story" itself.

Douglas's instinct, drawn from his commitment both to the Gospel and to that Gospel's Lord, have always been widely drawn. Like John Wesley before him, he regarded the world as his parish, and knew no limit of creed, colour or nationality. That for me is ecumenism as it should be in today's Church, where the urge to inter-faith dialogue is the requirement of the 21st Century.

I believe that Douglas Lister would share this opinion. In that spirit of enthusiastic Christ-driven humanity, he has written a memorable story. I commend it to you.

Maxwell Craig.
Queen's Chaplain, Stirling.

"It is at once moving, entertaining and spirited. A marvellous read."
Norman Harper, *Aberdeen Press and Journal.*

"A marvellously entertaining and worthwhile story, told with great style."
Ron Ferguson, *Freelance Journalist.*

iii

Biographical Notes

The author was born and brought up on the Island of Bute; educated at Rothesay Academy; Glasgow University: 1938-1941, Master of Arts (Junior Honours - English and Greek): Trinity Theological College, Glasgow 1941-1944, Bachelor of Divinity, Royal Army Chaplains Department: 1945-1949, Glasgow, Gibraltar, Germany. Minister of St. Stephen's Church, Carnoustie 1949-1955. Chaplain to "The Suez Contractors Ltd.," The Canal Zone, Egypt. On six year Contract, 13 January 1956, terminated 31st October 1956 with arrest and Imprisonment in Cairo. Minister, St. Andrews Church, Inverurie 1957-1967. Minister, Largo and Newburn Parish Church, Largo, Fife, 1967-1986, Retired 31st October 1986. Honorary Assistant - St. Machar's Cathedral, Aberdeen 1990-1993.

Publications: Book "Largo Kirk" 1968.
Columnist: East Fife Mail, Johnston Press, Leven, Inverurie Advertiser, Turriff.

Luneburg. On 4th May 1945, on Luneburg Heath Field Marshall Bernard Montgomery accepted the "unconditional surrender" of Germany; marking the end of the Second Word War. The town of Luneburg nearby, with its 65,000 citizens, is situated between Hamburg and Hanover in North Germany.

Acknowledgement

"This is a great story!" said Alan Grant, Chief Executive of Gordon District, when the story of "A Street in Luneburg" first saw the light of day (1996). "You should write it up." I have written it up now. In doing so I wish to thank my wife Sandra, for her encouragement. I am grateful too for the help of Bill Murdoch, James Mackay, Douglas Prosser and Algy Watson in reading and criticising the Script. And I am indebted to Maxwell Craig for writing the Foreword. I hope all who read "The Luneburg Story" will enjoy it.

Douglas Lister,
"Gowan Bank"
Port Elphinstone
Inverurie AB51 3UN
Tel. 01467 621262
Email: pastellister@surf-scotland.net

Douglas Lister, 1945

Marion, 1945

Contents

Chapter 1

GERMANY CALLING

My posting for insubordination in 1946 was the best posting I was ever to have. I was in Gibraltar as Garrison Chaplain. Stationed high up on the Rock I lived with the Liverpool Scottish Regiment and acted as Minister of the Church of Scotland in the town square.

I wasn't long there, when a colleague and friend, John Birkbeck asked me, if I could raise money for the Commando Benevolent Fund. John had been Chaplain of the 9 Commando throughout the war. I had met some of No. 9 Commando in Bute, where they had done some of their training. I had admired them and many like them.

With some of the troops who gathered often for social evenings in the Manse at 29, Scud Hill, we launched the Campaign for the Commandos. The Gibraltarians, showed their appreciation for the sacrifices of others that had clearly benefited them. They responded generously.

Half way through the appeal I received a letter from the Brigadier in charge asking me to stop. He had been asked to raise money for the Army Benevolent Fund. I compromised on the matter, but evidently not enough for the Brigadier, not nearly enough. I was due for a Posting!

"Would you like to go to Germany as Garrison Chaplain to 5000 Service Personnel, in Luneburg, and attached to The Royal Scots Greys?" asked the Army Chaplains Department. "Yes, that would be something different" I replied. It was! Being with "The Greys" was great, and the work hard but worthwhile. I formed friendships then that have lasted a lifetime.

It was 1947 in the desolation and hopelessness of post war Germany. Their great cities and towns lay in ruins around them, as ours did, as a result of the war's "obliterative bombing." Poverty and hunger were everywhere around along with the guilt of having been conned, as we were, by Adolf Hitler. At the same time the majority of them welcomed us as liberators from tyranny. Our Normandy forces had advanced to Luneburg by the River Elbe. On the other side of the river, there were the Russians. The Luneburg people felt that in us they had been given a double deliverance. In fact under the Yalta Agreement made with Stalin by

1

Churchill and Roosevelt, the Russians were to have gone more than a hundred and fifty miles further West as well as to occupy most of the Balkan Countries.

In 1947 Europe was in the middle of the worst winter of the Century. Hard, hard frost, mountains of snow; and dark miserable days didn't make for great pleasure.

One day, my secretary, Marion Niemeyer said, "There's a gentleman who would like to speak to you Douglas."

To Marion's news of a visitor, I replied, "Ask our friend to come in."

I can see him yet. He was thin and tall, a long gangling figure of a man. He wore a leather Luftwaffe jacket. On his chest hung a camera. His name was Joseph Makovec. "Call me Mac," he said. He had been a Bomber Pilot during the war. He was a professional photographer. Along with Marion and many others he simply wanted to help put together again the lives of the people he loved. I didn't know it at the time, but he had been accepted by John Chaloner, Field Marshall Montgomery's Press Aide, to serve in his corps for the new Germany.

"I wonder if you can possibly help us?" he asked with some anguish in his voice. "There are 80,000 Refugees out there, freezing to death. A year ago they fled from the Russian Zone across the nearby River Elbe." "I have over 5,000 souls here to try and care for," I replied. "I know," said Mac. "What can I do?" I countered. I remember the slightly quizzical smile on his face as he replied "You could perhaps get them to help too."

I hadn't known anyone teach me my own job so well before. I realised we were the same kind of people and we bonded at that moment and were to stay that way.

We went down together to see the Refugees. Mile upon mile in the fields by the river Elbe was an encampment of old army tents; a city of the lost. In the gathering dusk we went into the tents. There was no furniture of any kind, beds made up of old blankets were on the floors. A rickety old stove in the corner on which cabbage was being boiled, the smell of which I've never forgotten. In the tents were very old and weary men and women, young fine looking couples and often on the freezing floor, new-born babies wrapped in old newspapers - all they had for blankets and nappies.

Horrified by what I saw. I knew I had to help and decided to do so. With my new-found friend, Jo Makovec we laid our plans. I applied for

2

permission to the High Command, but they said "No!" "Non-Fraternisation with the Enemy" is the "Order of the Day!"

This left me very angry. I knew there was a case for "non fraternisation with the enemy" in the interest of order and peace, but I knew this was different.

In the evening I discussed it over a drink in the Mess with a very good friend, Captain John Althorp. I knew nothing at all about John's background or personal life. It didn't matter to either of us. We simply got on well together. We knew we were on the same wavelengths of need, hope and trust. We were relaxed and at peace with each other. John was just a wonderful person to be with. Soon after I had come to the Greys, John had sought me out. His hopes and dreams had been seriously and sadly dashed. His love for and hopes to marry Princess Elizabeth had been overturned. In great sadness and in deep sincerity he shared his grief. I myself was profoundly upset by what he told me. I could not have imagined a better person to be Consort to the Queen. I never told another of what we had shared that night.

I needed him now. He knew it, and rose to the occasion as he always did. I was never to forget John's reaction. Angry too, he said, "Good God. These poor people are no enemies! Fight the High Command."

I decided to do so. My letter to the high command was "As my order as Chaplain is to serve people regardless of race, colour or in my opinion religion I wish to appeal against the rule in question. I consider it my duty to help those people in their need if I possibly can. I would be grateful if you could give me permission to do so."

I was lucky in that I had to work through the Brigadier of 4th Armoured Brigade stationed in Luneburg, Rex de Winton. After discussion with him Rex a very fine and fair-minded man answered "Go ahead Douglas and may God bless these good people."

Jo Makovec and I composed an appeal giving the facts of the case. I was to discover fifty years later that another hand was behind it all. Appointed with Jo by John Chaloner, Montgomery's aide in establishing the new Germany, one Helmut Pless was editor of the Luneburg Landezeitung "No 3 in the free press of liberated Germany." Together they were proof of the wisdom of our authorities in building on the trust and co-operation of the German people toward the allied invasion troops.

The letter, which I sent out all over Scotland, was as follows:

3

Germany Calling

AN APPEAL FOR YOUR HELP

MY DEAR FRIEND,   Luneburg Summer 1947.

I am sending you this appeal from this ancient and very beautiful town of Luneburg in North Germany. It has been less seriously affected by the War than most places, but even so the scarcity is appalling, the need is desperate. Further, we are near to other places, once magnificent cities, now heaps of hopeless rubble, Hamburg, Hanover and Munster. More than two years have passed since we occupied this land. We have had great and heavy responsibilities at home and abroad, and perhaps as a result of this conditions here have not improved but deteriorated. Now Germany stands in a very dangerous position, physically, morally and spiritually. She is needing widescale help immediately. And one thing is certain; IF SHE GETS IT SHE WILL BELIEVE IN US, RESPOND, AND WORK WITH US IN EUROPE'S DIFFICULT FUTURE. Of this I am thoroughly convinced.

We who are in Germany are trying to build up trust and co-operation as best we can. But the people's need is overwhelming and our ability to help is very small. It is because of this I am sending you this appeal – which I ask you to believe is urgent and truthful. We must help our administration in Germany all we can, but the direct way of saving, or at least helping the situation, is for each of us, as individuals or as a group to play our part. By your own effort, your Church and minister, your Youth club campaign and other ways, you can help, and I am sure will. In this way you will be helping a brother in really desperate need, you will be helping our Government here, you will be relieving the position in Europe and in a true sense, safeguarding the future existence of your children.

In the remainder of this leaflet you will read more of the situation and of ways in which you can help. But believe me when I say we must do what we can at once. Winter is approaching; and from reliable reports, it will be very severe and difficult. All that we can do here, and the support we receive from you at home will be most valuable; nowhere more appreciated than by the poor and needy people of this district.

I send this letter to you in complete confidence that you will co-operate, and recruit others in this campaign, and thus make it a success far greater than we could ever expect.

I am, Yours very sincerely,

DOUGLAS LISTER C.F.

The "Germany Calling" Appeal we sent all over Scotland brought in many tons of top quality food and clothing. I was overwhelmed by Scotland's generosity. It however spoke volumes about Scotland and her people that I was to discover later in over 50 years of Ministry. Deeds, rather than words are their currency and strength.

But always too, I was to remember the encouragement of John Althorp, later to become Earl Spencer, and father of Diana, Princess of Wales. His genuine feeling for the oppressed, which so obviously surfaced in his daughter; and the injunction, where cruel injustice and inhumanity are at stake, as they often are, "Fight the High Command" - is the right thing to do, regardless of the consequences. Of course there was sense in the general observance of the rule, in its intention of preserving and. aiding social peace. There often is good reason for most rules. But there is always good reason for judging them critically. Unthinking acceptance and obedience can often allow abuse and injustice to proceed unchecked.

The "Germany Calling" Appeal that Jo Makovec and I sent all over Scotland had brought in tons of top quality food and clothes. The response itself had taken us and Luneburg by surprise. And to me, there was added mystery. All of it came anonymously. One post-mark, on a weekly consignment of absolutely wonderful goods fascinated us.

The postmark on the parcels, was SCALLOWAY. Somewhere in the far and beautiful Islands of the Shetlands. "Some day," I said to Marion, my wife- "We should go to Shetland, and try and unravel this rather lovely mystery!"

"THE SPIRIT OF SCALLOWAY"
"The Shetland Bus"

Twenty seven years later, we decided to go to visit Bill and Mary Dodd. who had left Keithall by Inverurie to serve as Lay Missionaries in Sandwick, Shetland. We stayed with a charming Shetlander Emma Nicholson." Where is Scalloway?" I asked her. "A few miles over the hill" she replied. "Let's go to Scalloway, and find out who the 'secret people' were," I said to Marion.

I asked a man by the harbour. "Try Jack Moore," he suggested. "But mind, Jack and Peg, lost their son, a fortnight ago, drowned in the harbour, caught in some cabling."

Jack and Peg welcomed us most courteously. "Yes, I think I can help you," said Jack. I serviced the ships of "The Shetland Bus," during the War. "The Shetland Bus" was the name given to this hazardous and daring rescue mission that brought supplies to men and women in need.

The ships and crews involved risked their lives from often mountainous seas and appaling conditions, not to speak of German U.Boats and Destroyers who had learned of their operation for Norwegian and British personnel. Jack quietly added "I decided to give part of my Contract Fees to the W.R.V.S., to use as they thought right. They received your "Germany Calling" leaflet from somewhere and decided to support you."

So the essential spirit of Scalloway had lived on, caring for people in desperate straits regardless of conventional labels and creed. And characteristically it was all done "anonymously!"

I was never to forget the people of Scalloway, and their "anonymous" Aid. Their help and that of thousands of others whose names we never knew saved the lives of hundreds of "enemies" in their hour of need. And, in many difficult and dark times in the years ahead, I was to remember the tears, smiles and thanks of hundreds of refugees, as we left for home.

In fact, other chaplains across Europe had also been helping people in their difficulties, this developed into what was named "Inter Church and Refugee Service." "Christian Aid" grew out of this to become one of the most important and useful operations of the Christian Church.

Chapter 2

A STREET IN LUNEBURG

Makovec and I kept Christmas Card contact. In 1966, I wrote him telling that we were going on a motoring holiday to Switzerland and would like to return by Luneburg to see him, his wife Lisel and perhaps Marion Niemeyer who had been my Secretary. That return was to be full of surprises, unexpected and pleasant. My diary for Monday and Tuesday September 12th and 13th 1966 describes some of them:-

"To Luneburg; where we learn that Rotary and Ratsherren were waiting for us. Joe Makovec responsible. The Council have given us rooms at the Stadt Hamburg Hotel by St. John's in the Am Sande. Such a welcome we never dreamt of. It is moving after 18 years, to be remembered and received and written up in the local Paper like this. It is marvellous to be one with these old friends again." And on the Tuesday:- "See over the Rathaus and are given a Civic Reception at the Ratskeller. Oberburgermeister Dr. Berchen Thanks me for the work of the "Germany Calling Appeal," 18 years

Jo & Lisel Makovec

before, and presents me with the bronze Seal of Luneburg. In the afternoon we go to Luneburge Heide. A wonderful time."

For all our good resolves to keep in touch, we did in fact lose touch. My wife Marion died of cancer on 10th May 1976, in 1987 I met and married Sandra and returned to live in Inverurie.

On a Wednesday in July 1995 a young German lawyer, Klaus Schultse of Wiesbaden was addressing our Probus Club on "Europe." While he spoke I found myself thinking of Jo and Lisel Makovec, wondering if they might still be alive. Klaus helped me write a letter to the Oberburgermeister of Luneburg enquiring to that effect. The letter received an affirmative reply.

Mac and Lisel Makovec were alive and well. Mac's first letter (15/7/95.) said "What a surprise to check my answering machine and hear a voice say "Do you remember Douglas Lister Mr Makovec?" Must I express our joy to hear from you after such a long time! We feel very sorry that your dear wife Marion has died. Lisel remembers her giving her a pair of the then precious nylons and much love beside. I have to tell you that the town council concluded to name one of the new streets should bear your name. We could not trace you but they named the street in the west end of the town 'Douglas Lister Strasse' by order of the town council 30 May 1991.

Then one evening a Mr Jack Campbell of Aberdeen Rotary telephoned "I have a letter here which might interest you. May I send you a copy?" "Yes, of course" I replied. It was a letter the head of Rotary U.K. Mr Mike Redfern had received.

Dear Mr Redfern

I am writing to you on behalf of Mr Pless, editor-in-chief of DER ROTARIER, to ask for help in trying to find out the address of a British Rotarian Padre Douglas Lister who right after World War II, and despite all talk against fraternisation, decided to help the Germans in Luneburg by bringing hope and bread, and other things of help. Mr Pless would like to get into contact with him, and since he is supposedly a Rotarian in Aberdeen thought that you might help him obtaining the address.

Yours sincerely

Katrin Lilienthal

I wrote to Mr Pless informing him that I was the guilty party and still alive!

On Christmas Eve a crisp, cold morning I received one of the best Christmas cards I had ever known. It was from Luneburg, it read:

Dear Padre Lister

Like Bethlehem miracles take their own time to happen. And they take their own time to remind people that they happened in centuries, years and days gone by. That's what I felt receiving your letter. It reminded me to a miracle of humanity and unselfishness and individual courage, that enlightened a candle of hope to refugees, displaced and troubled people in post war Luneburg. You may already know, that people here still remember the sign of hope you established in their heart and they named a street after Padre Lister.

Helmut Pless

Interested and, of course, pleased, we thought of going out to Luneburg to meet "our friends" again, and have a wee "peek" at "The Street." "The Scotsman" was advertising half-price sailings to Hamburg on "Scandinavian Seaways," on supply of Vouchers.

We were on the point of sending off our Vouchers, when a letter arrived from a Dr Joachim Engelhardt International Convener, for Rotary Luneburg inviting Sandra and myself to be with them as Guests of Honour at the 40th Anniversary Celebrations of Luneburg's Rotary.

We accepted - with pleasure! Fortune not always so kind! A deputation met us at Hamburg Airport; a "Lister" placard was held aloft among the crowd. "Some celebrity or other" I remarked to Sandra. "It looks like it" she laughed. Among the Group I met for the first time was Helmut Pless.

Helmut Pless

Helmut Pless, a much decorated former Luftwaffe Pilot and editor of "Der Rotarier," the Rotary Magazine for Germany and Austria. Helmut, we discovered had been involved with Jo in the original "Germany Calling" Appeal; and very much so in the naming of "The Street." Helmut and Magda Pless, like Jo and Lisel Makovec devoted their lives to the ways of reconciliation and peace. It was privilege and joy to be now one with them.

We arrived in Luneburg on May 9th "Europe Day" and, in the loveliness of "Paradise"-woods by the Heath of Luneburg, we quietly walked and dined with our friends.

On the second day, the City Fathers and Council met and honoured us in the beautiful "Rathaus." Thanks were said. A Scroll presented I replied, returning thanks, bringing good wishes from "The Church of Scotland," the "Greys," the "Inverurie and Aberdeen Rotary Clubs," and Gordon Council, and my friend Brian Pack, General Manager of Aberdeen and Northern Marts. The B.S.E. crisis was raging in Europe at the time.

Realising that all I said and did was going to be broadcast across Germany as it was I not only offered greetings but in invitation to come to Scotland and particularly Aberdeenshire where they would meet the finest people in the world in a beautiful land and perhaps taste our liquid gold - whisky. "You now have, however, a street with the wrong name, it should have been named Marion Strasse. My wife Marion was the main encourager and inspiration then as always."

At that point I happened to glance down at the Scroll of Honour in my hand "10th May, 1996." It was to the day, hour, minute - 10th May 1976, twenty years exactly, since June Ford, the sweet little Nurse in Ward 14, phoned me to say, gently, "Douglas, Marion has just died!" It all came back, and Marion with it. It stopped me in my tracks, for a good eight seconds; which felt like minutes. But I was glad to have her so near again.

So I received the Silver Medal for Distinguished Service; signed the Golden Book (the prior signature of 1995 was, David Montgomery, son of Field Marshall Montgomery. He had been invited out and honoured by the City on the 50th Anniversary of the signing of the Unconditional Surrender of Germany, by his Father at Luneburg Heath.

In good company we ate and drank together, as though friends for life; it was lovely and we were just at home.

Next day, was to be the big one. In the historic great Hall of Luneburg, the Princes and Princesses of the House of Hanover, looking down from the beautiful murals; and five hundred Rotarians from all over Europe the audience. Strangely enough, I felt as calm and happy as when I first used to take Marion out cycling along the roads or walking round the lochs of Bute. President Kay Von Wedel welcomed and addressed the guests; and presented me with the Scroll, appointing me the 1st Honorary Member of Luneburg Rotary. It records that "stationed at the Schliefen Barracks from 1947-49, Douglas Lister, unselfishly and in defiance of all orders, which threatened severe punishment of all "fraternization" rendered Christian aid and devoted great effort to international understanding. Faced with the distress of the

Sandra and David with German officials

refugees, and repatriates in the hopelessly, overcrowded town of Luneburg, launched the "Germany Calling" appeal in Scotland, a humanitarian relief campaign which enabled food, clothing and medicine to be distributed to the needy." That was nice. But a bit much. Anyway it was the anonymous people in Scotland who did it and deserved the praise. But at least we helped a little. And it was appreciated; and still is fifty years on.

The Guest Speaker was the German Federal Minister of Justice, Dr Edzard Schmidt-Jortzig. He spoke on "Europe"-almost Churchill speaking "We need each other. We ought to help each other. Let's do it as fairly, helpfully and unitedly as we can."

Before his main speech, he addressed me personally. "Mr Lister, I was a young boy here in Luneburg, when you did your great work. I was very impressed. We all were. We always remembered. Now, on my own, and on Germany's behalf we thank you." Of course it was all a great honour and pleasure, and I was and am grateful. Especially for rather wonderful friendships renewed and made.

On the Sunday I was, privileged to share the service in the great St. Joahannes Kirche, where we used to gather and worship with our British congregations. The retired Superintendent Martin Voigt shared the service. In the congregation was the son of my old friend Pastor Achim Puschmann; Wolfgang, now Superintendent of the Church in Hanover.

In the afternoon. Martin took Sandra and I out to Victory Hill. Field Marshall Montgomery had erected a great Victory Memorial on the site. It had been stolen a year later and never recovered. On its place is now a simple red granite block with the words "1939-1945. No More War."

"Where were you during the War? I asked Martin Voigt.

"I was in Celle. Celle is a very beautiful small town south of Luneburg. My father was the Pastor. We rather lived in fear of our lives. He was very anti-Nazi and he preached openly against Hitler.

From time to time a high ranking Gestapo Officer would come to the Manse. He lectured my father that if he continued to preach so openly against Hitler, not only he, but the whole family would likely be arrested and taken to a Prison Camp. A few days after the end of the War, a tall, well spoken English Officer came to the Manse. "Could I perhaps see your

Father?" he asked. "Yes" we said happily. In father's study, the Officer said. "We have met before Pastor Voigt." "No, we haven't my father replied. "Turn round for a moment" said the Officer. "Thank you" "Turn again," said the Officer. My father was looking at the high ranking Gestapo Officer, who had warned him during the War. The English Officer had been a spy, who visited Pastors and others, who were known to be against Hitler, and in danger of their lives."

Martin and his wife Helga are lovely people. I'm glad we managed to save their lives and that of many many others, who were at heart or even openly supporters of a better future for all of Europe.

But for me the most moving moments, by far, were meeting, speaking to and getting to know a group of the grandchildren of the refugees we had been able to help 50 years before. They were a group of most marvellous young people; and all of them enthusiastic about Scotland and European Unity.

As we met, I remembered the terrible times of 1947, and their grandparents. I saw them again - little new born things, on the cold ground, wrapped in old newspapers, all they had for blankets and nappies. I was grateful for the many, many good people of Scotland, who had decided to do something for those people in Germany. It had been worthwhile.

Chapter 3

I SHOULD NOT HAVE BEEN BORN

It may not be unusual now, but in the 20's it was slightly different.

As I surfaced into life at 4.20 p.m. on 5 July 1920 at 8 Auchnacloich Road, Rothesay, I knew something was wrong, I was not to discover how wrong till later. But I sensed it through every pore.

How soon does "feeling" begin in a living soul? I wonder if we shall ever know? I think there is little doubt that "atmosphere," "sensation" and more, make themselves felt in our consciousness from the beginning, whenever that is.

I did not know, and was not to know till years later, that something of the tragic irony of life was taking place in the ticking of the clock in the room, where midwife Helen Wilson was delivering me. She was delivering two babies - the issue of two sisters. One sister, Margaret, was unmarried and fervently hoping and praying not to have her child. The other sister, Alice, with her husband, was looking forward to having and holding in her arms their longed for son and heir.

I was born fit and well "a nice child." My cousin was delivered half an hour later beside me "a very lovely boy" - still born. An hour of real sorrow and tragedy in an ordinary house - in 1920.

Little wonder I sensed the wrongness of things. My uncle longing for a son was heart broken. A proud and ambitious businessman he was never to forgive my mother or myself. I should not have been born, his son should. Always there was tension in the air. Whenever he appeared I was discreetly moved out of sight.

Alice and her husband Jack had kindly decided not to move to Glasgow, had sacrificed their future in a family extended in distress and pain. A sister disgraced when disgrace was real, their son dead. They were at the heart of life's cruel fate and daily bitterness and a tiny waif at its centre.

Uncle Jack commuted daily by steamer to the mainland Wemyss Bay; and by train to Glasgow to his slater and plasterer's business in Waddell Street in the Gorbals returning by the same route after his day's work in the evening to Rothesay. An arduous and energy sapping life and a real struggle in the twenties. Of course I didn't know or understand anything of that. And, as with other children the strange, and at times, distressing expressions of it, I was more sensitive of it, than was perhaps good for me. I came to understand and respect the meaning of them later; and to try and build a sensible relationship with my Uncle, but it is difficult to restore bridges of affection that have been so surely fractured in the rebuffs of our earliest years.

I was to learn later, too, that the young, and trusted Family Doctor, Dr. Penney, summoned by the Midwife to attend the births, on July 5th, had suggested the children should perhaps be switched; so that my Aunt should have the child she longed to have, and my Mother relieved of her unwanted child. Grandma Lister, quiet, stately, dressed always in black, understanding the doctor's social concern, intervened. "I think, Doctor, if you don't mind, we should accept our lot." That agreed, so it was.

I often think of the Grandmother, whose death eight years later, greatly distressed me. We often know so little about our Grandparents. I did not know, that two years before my unwelcome impending arrival, her oldest son, Alex had died rather mysteriously in Boston, in the United States; nor that her husband had died less than a year before. The extended family into which I had arrived had been a caring and noble one. I owed much more to that "cradling" than many others like me.

For her part, my mother - I had to call her Aunt Margaret worked hard to build up her business, double burdened indeed in the twenties. Struggling for survival in business and unmarried with a child. At home Grandma Lister, quiet, dignified and calm, gave what help she could, and Alice "Aunt Alice" I now realise treated me as the child she lost. In her, I now recognise, I was a very fortunate child.

When I was really frightened and trying not to show it, it was in her that I found refuge, comfort and hope. I was sometimes desperate for these and would quietly go to her and find in the warmth of her embrace the help for which I was yearning.

Yet, as often the case, some things hurt and quite badly. I had to sleep with my mother. If ever I stretched out for her she moved my hand and quietly placed it back where it had been. That, I used to feel was something wrong for me to do. I never received a hug of affection from her. Somehow she was either unwilling or unable to show her love. How often we do not understand the meaning of things.

One thing I simply hated was being dressed up and taken round at weekends as though on show. I remember the feeling of cringing inside. But what else could she do, what else could a hard worked and rather lonely mother do. When I could, I escaped. I remember one Sunday I was out with boys, I fell into the Lover's Walk lane sailing sticks as boats down the rapids of the stream. Stretching too far, I fell into the water. It took hours of running to dry my Sunday suit before going home. On another day I slipped out of the kitchen of James Mackay's "Barone Park" farm. A plank beckoned, I walked the plank, wobbled, fell off and into a very large soft midden. My cries for help led to my being dragged out very dirty and smelly. It meant the end of my new blue suit as I was hosed down in very cold water. It was the most wonderful baptism I ever remember having.

When I was about seven or eight and feeling confused and lost, I plucked up courage to ask my mother "Why am I different from everybody else?" Four times I asked her, four times she answered in precisely the same words "I sinned and you are the fruit of my sins." It didn't help, it didn't help at all, but I never asked again. I simply resolved to make it on my own.

In my early teens I resolved most definitely that handicapped or not, I would make a go of things on my own and from then on I set out to do that. I was to find that it was not as easy to do as I thought.

I was part of an extended family of twenty or so. I so longed to belong. But I never felt I did. I was to find myself fighting on several fronts at the same time.

Not meant to be alive, I wanted to live. The result of sex that was wrong, I wanted to love and be able to make love. Counting for little I wanted to have some significance.

I tried hard to make it. At University, I still remember, standing still, and sweating, profusely at filling up endless forms- "Father's Name; Father's Profession - Mother's Maiden Name. Especially then, I would have given almost anything to have been, as the other boys and girls were.

I don't know how it is for boys and girls in my situation now; but that's how it was then. I fear today's young have terrors quite as great if not worse. Traumas can go terribly deep and last all too long.

In 1954 and 1955, standing in the pulpit of Iona Abbey, I looked at a finely sculptured face on the arch opposite, picture of a soul in agony. I was looking at myself. I glanced at the congregations, and saw others like me.

As a boy I had loved the story of Robert the Bruce's friend and companion in arms, Sir James Douglas. On his deathbed, Bruce asked Douglas to carry on his battle for justice and freedom. Sir James carried Bruce's heart embalmed in a silver casket wherever he went. On his way to

Jerusalem, finding himself hopelessly outnumbered in fierce battle, he turned to face and fight the enemy, crying at the top of his voice "Forward, Braveheart Douglas will follow thee, or die!" He died in battle.

My days were to be marked with something of that recklessness, but less of its valour and wisdom.

In February 1963, I had ended a busy day of Communion. Over 1400 members had received the Sacrament. Tired but happy I opened the Manse door, "Your Mother's been taken into Greenock Hospital, Dear," said my wife, Marion. "She's very ill." After a quick snack, I motored the 150 miles to be with her. She was glad to see me. She was calm and brave. A few days later she died. Her face was beautiful and at peace. I'd never seen her like that. Through unbidden sobs, I heard myself say, "It wasn't her fault."

On 10th May 1976, the best wife a man could have, Marion died of cancer. I was a lost soul. For a long time, depression that recurred I found difficult to handle.

On 22nd May 1987 "The Day I met Sandra" the difficult pieces of my life's jigsaw, quietly slipped into place. Words were not needed. We both knew. I was at peace. I knew I had arrived where all my life I'd longed to be. I was home where I had desperately wanted to be. I was impossibly grateful and am still.

I had not, of course, enjoyed being illegitimate or experiencing some of the consequences, which seemed to flow from it. Certainly I did not like anything of the serious and dangerous life threatening depression that I knew in mid life and afterwards.

But I was to discover that I was not alone. Compared with millions of others I was lucky. Need takes many forms. It is right to feel for the needs of others. It is wise to accept help when need is great. There are many who count it a privilege to be a friend to a neighbour in need. The joy of being helped and especially of helping others even in a small way, is perhaps one of the most precious things life can hold.

On a beautiful July day, in the attractive setting of Pittodrie House Hotel, under the shadow of Aberdeenshire's beautiful mountain, Bennachie, Sandra and I celebrated my 77th birthday. I was surprised to find myself raise my glass and say with spontaneous feeling "Here's to my mother!" It was the first time I had toasted her on my birthday. It is a pity that it can take so long sometimes to pay tribute to those who have loved us.

Chapter 4

THE LOVELY ISLAND

I couldn't have been luckier to be born in Rothesay and brought up among its people on the lovely island of Bute in the Firth of Clyde. Bute was to become for me a kind of second Iona. It was of course created on the Eighth Day.

The Reverend Alistair Maclean father of writer Alistair Maclean of HMS Ulysses, Ice Station Zebra fame used to say "God rested on the seventh day, well pleased with His works, but on the eighth day He felt something deep inside His robes It was a cluster of jewels, beautiful diamonds. The Lord looked down and seeing the sun shining on a clear stretch of water He scattered the jewels and where they settled into the waters there was created the Western Isles and He called them the Hebrides." What Mr Maclean didn't know was that a few of the diamonds were caught on a gentle breeze and blown south and kissed the sunshine on the seas of the Clyde. So it came to be that on the eighth day Buteshire and its islands of Arran the Cumbrae and Bute itself were made. Bute is a tiny island 15 miles long by 5 miles wide. Small, but of great beauty of fields and hills, lochs and sandy beaches.

The past is always around the natives and visitors alike. It's a feeling in the air. Stones that have stood for thousands of years, pieces of castles, the leavings of houses put down by islanders who had come from Ireland, France and Spain before Christianity was ever known.

They liked what they found and stayed. Many burial sites of Bronze Age times (C2500 - C500 BC) show quite a large population on the island then. The past is round the feet of all who live on the island and the thousands of visitors who walk its intriguing and varied ways and moors, round its sandy or rocky and heather covered shores. There's history, mystery, bloodshed and beauty of the past and present all the way in Bute.

Rothesay Castle, the seat of Viking chiefs and kings in more recent times, was first built on a mound on the edge of the sea. Until the Duke of Argyll burned it in the 17th century it played its part in the tidal wars of Viking, Scots and English as in the rest of Britain. Edward I of England (Langshanks) Scourge of Scotland and enemy forever as a result laid the island waste in his revengeful way. Rothesay has been "Royal" since 1400 when Robert III granted it his charter. But the true royal part of Rothesay is its people. In my youth it was always known as Royal Rothesay, and so it was.

The sea views are breathtaking in their beauty. Vantage points tell their own stories from far above its bay, Rothesay Bay, beautiful as Naples. The curvaceous beauty of the Bay and the lovely Kyles of Bute, between the North of the Island and the mainland of Argyll can best be seen and enjoyed from high above the town, on Canada Hill, looking down on the River Clyde.

Its seascape opens up to what were the great shipyards of the Clyde and down to the open sea, Ireland and the Atlantic. A seaway for thousands of years. Of recent years hundreds of thousands victims of the Highland Clearances, fortune and adventure seekers sailed from it to Canada and their Nova Scotia. From the waters of the Clyde thousands of Clyde-built ships have set out on their voyages of discovery and conquest.

My favourite spot was in the southwest tip of the island, there, tucked in a sheltered spot is St. Blanes. The view is breathtaking - across a wide stretch of the Clyde, where for long, on "The Measured Mile" the great Clyde-Built ships of the line - naval and merchant - were tested for their speed and other capabilities - and beyond the magic Island of Arran topped by its "Sleeping Warrior" and Goatfell appears silhouetted against the sky.

"St. Blane" was one of the early missionaries who came from Ireland with their "Gospel for Scotland." They were to leave their mark etched indelibly on the land, people and soul of Scotland, for good. They loved the whole of Scotland, body and soul; and Scotland has not forgotten them. Not least of their charm was that they were seafaring people too, adventurers all. Bute was to choose Brendan, the Sailor, as its champion. Natives of Bute are called "Brandanes, St. Brendan's people. An open-air service in the setting of St. Blane's early community at the south west of Bute, was one of the gatherings I enjoyed as a boy. That sort of link with our past, I liked, and like.

From early 20th century Bute was well served by very fine and beautiful paddle steamers and good rail connections. It became a commuter's paradise and residence for many of the better off. It was an ideal holiday island and in my time during the Glasgow Fair Fortnight it was full to overflowing with holidaymakers and their children. They took over Rothesay as their home, their loud West Coast but unmistakable long broad vowelled Glasgow accents and gusty laughter resonating and echoing in every street and from every close. Glasgow had come to town. Natives had no right to move. I often found it useless trying to cycle with a message bike packed with goods through the seething herds of raucous Glaswegians. I often had to get off my bike and push. There was something infectious about the carefree, generous open-minded happiness of the Glasgow crowds. They gave all they could to make "Doon the watter" holidays of a life time for their families. They went home "broke," every penny spent, their cup of happy merriment bubbling over on steamer and train till the taxi reached the tenement. Upstairs they took the "half crown piece" from the jug on the mantelpiece, paid the taxi and started from scratch, penniless till next July.

When the war came in 1939 the Glasgow folk were gone, never to return, at least until now.

The town was filled to overflowing with service personnel. The Navy was everywhere - "The Cyclops" supply ship, warships, destroyers, mini submarines and landing crafts. Later there came Canadians, No. 9 Commando and the Polish invasion that was to change Scotland for good.

The fine young men of Bute were gone too, on to St Valery, retreating from Dunkirk, re-grouping and back again; lost at sea and in the air, captured at Tobruk, forgotten in Burma's forests, prisoners at "Changi." Brave and mostly cheerful they were; many fortunately back home and glad; their work done and begun.

Personally I realise there were several straws in the wind.

Being sent to my room when very young. Visitors had criticised people in new council houses "These sort of folk will only put coal in their baths." I exploded "Don't talk rot. I've a friend Jimmy Boyle. He and his parents are as good as you. In fact I think better."

One Christmas Eve I remember cycling up the steep Serpentine Hill with my basket filled with goods. It was nearly midnight. We worked till midnight and after in those days; particularly at Christmas-time. I loved working in the shop helping my mother, meeting people and taking good quality parcels, which I think I regarded as gifts to them. I had learned by then the cost of things. I knew my mother insisted on quality and considerate service. I knew too that, if I'd been in charge I would have charged quite a bit more than she chose to do.

That night as I puffed happily up the steep hill, Trinity Church bells began to ring in Castle Street below. First I wondered why, then I remembered. It was the first Christmas Eve Carol Service to be held in the town. I remember thinking "Good, that's nice." Then even more certainly, "I think that what I'm doing now is as good and important as what's going on in church." I've never changed my opinion on that.

Then again I remember my mother used to employ an interesting and whiskered gentleman to do repair work in the shop "He's quite the best joiner in the town," she said. Then she would send me with my basket packed with goodies to take round to him. I loved meeting him. He had such a gentle, kind face and musical voice. His little house and everything in it was a sort of sooty black. I felt so much at home with him that we often would sit down and we'd talk for ages. This old man and youngster, heart to heart. I've never forgotten him Tom Bowman was his name. I soon realised the reason why he was paid in goods and not cash. He was an alcoholic and like most alcoholics I've known he was sensitive and lonely and somehow hurt. I never of course found out why, but I felt I understood. I loved the man.

Then again there was someone who influenced me greatly, he was Provost of the town, owner of a fine shoe shop - Angus Thomson. In a fairly large congregation he was superintendent of a Bible Class of one. He took the class every Sunday in a most intelligent, courteous and interesting way. I was the only one. I think he had more to do than anyone in my ending up a minister of the Church of Scotland.

Bute has had many distinguished residents. A recent one is Sir Richard Attenborough. He has been and is a protagonist for justice and mercy greater than many ministers have sometimes been.

The academy on the hill looking over the bay was a fine school and seat of liberal education. Music was wonderful. Pappa Gregory, complete with bow tie and long straggly black hair, was our unconventional teacher. The songs we gladly sang along with him were Tannhauser's "Pilgrim Chorus," William Blake's "Jerusalem" and Elgar's "Land of hope and glory." They have sung their way with us down the years.

Sometimes we questioned what we were taught. As in History. We were told the Great War of 1914-1918 was a great victory. Many in our Class had lost their fathers in its slaughter; some of the "lost generation" of Britain and Europe's Finest youth. We felt "The League of Nations" was a better way. On the other hand sometimes we welcomed our teaching. As in Geography. I remember Miss Duff pointing to a map of the world, a quarter of it coloured red. With pride she said "That quarter of the world is ours; our great British Empire!" We young Brandanes knew something of the might and majesty of Empire. Just a week before, three of the greatest battleships of the line, had sailed into Rothesay Bay and anchored proudly; H.M.S. Hood, H.M.S. Rodney and H.M.S. Nelson. We had been invited aboard H.M.S. Hood; escorted at speed across Rothesay Bay in naval pinnaces to the gigantic ship. Aboard we had walked the gleaming white decks, and, with fear, handled the huge thundering guns. This was Empire. Greatness that was ours that would never pass away. To feel, to think, otherwise was to be a traitor.

But after our youthful moment of glory, it was back to School; proud too of the education we enjoyed in Rothesay Academy.

I've just read in "The Scotsman" of the death of one of our Maths teachers. I can see and hear him still, very tall and with a head of frizzy dark Hair and a very gentle voice. He always seemed to have such great confidence in me. Perhaps it was because he knew that for all the front I put on, confidence was what I lacked most of all. My marks in Maths were abysmally bad. "Keep it up Douglas, you'll do well." He couldn't possibly mean at Maths. If I did well at anything, he and my other teachers had something quite real to do with it. A. M. Orr was his name. "Amo" we called him, Latin for "I love." He was that, a really nice man. He remained that happily, I was glad to hear till his death the other day at 103 years of age.

It helps to be born and brought up in a good place and among pleasant people.

Chapter 5

PADDLING INTO THE 21st CENTURY

For us as boys one of our happiest ploys and bits of fun was messing about in boats in Rothesay Bay. We hired a rowing boat from Dewars or McIvors Slips on the promenade and had an hour's freedom and joy far out into Rothesay Bay towards the Cowal shore. Yachts of various shapes and sizes would weave their way past us like angels dancing across the sea. We were not quite that class, but we were sailors in the great deep as they were.

But when the mistresses of the Clyde hoved into sight coming with their busy unmistakable beauty and pride we rowed like mad to meet them. The Clyde steamers whether on sunny days of splendour or when winds were high and white horses and spume whipped the sea into angry fury these Clyde heroines were our objects of delight and pride.

We rowed as close to them as possible leaning on our oars as they passed. We moved into the great waves of their wash as they rolled towards us and enjoyed being tossed to heaven and dipping down to hell.

What was the magic of the fleet of Clyde paddle steamers? It was a multi-faceted medley of wonder. They were extremely good looking; they had lines and features of deck, bridge, seating, saloons, funnels, smoke, masts and flags and engines of bright brass turning with a poetry of motion on to the happy sounding paddles that made them ride the waves well. For us passengers, we were proud to be with them at all times in idyllic calm or horrendous storm, willing our craft to reach pier or harbour successfully and in peace.

It was just a half hour's sail from Rothesay pier past Toward Point across the Clyde waterway to Wemyss Bay on the mainland, but each time it was a mini cruise under a good captain with an agreeable company. Cruising in the Clyde steamers was a cruise of a lifetime.

It all started on the Clyde in 1812 when the Comet, Europe's first commercial paddle steamer plied from Glasgow to Greenock, from then on the fleet of colourful steamers brought infinite pleasure to millions of travellers old and young and perhaps most going on holiday with their parents to the Clyde holiday resorts. There used to be a daily service from the Broomielaw in Glasgow to Rothesay. Highlights for that for me were the mystery tours that were run for the Rothesay Illuminations. The semi circle of Rothesay Bay was lit by millions of padella lights (little tins with wicks set in wax) - a sight of great beauty in itself and with illuminations above round the bay in the dark a kind of magic! Steamers would circle the bay looking for all the world as though they would capsize with thousands of merry carefree holiday travellers leaning on the rails towards the shore.

"Why has that ship got wheels?" asked a small boy as he saw the Waverley approach Rothesay pier. As she came into the pier and the huge paddles, frothing in their ornate black and gold mudguards, shuddered to a halt and went backwards, stopped in her tracks, side stepped and nuzzled gently against the dock "He put the brakes on!" said the small boy answering his own question.

That, in a word, represents the satisfaction and pride that the Clyde felt in her steamers.

Steamers have given place as our coastal transport to ferries for the present, but steamers are making a comeback. Like the others the Waverley was out of commission for a while. The Paddle Steamer Preservation Society paid a nominal £1 for the redundant Waverley in 1974 after her owners Caledonian MacBrayne decided she was too old, unreliable and expensive to run. She was like her sister ships, out of fashion, past her 'sail by date.' But her beauty, even on the scrap heap, wouldn't hide. The Preservation Society raised money to restore her. Restored and refitted, she is paddling enjoyably, usefully and beautifully as ever round Britain again.

In 1981 after conversion from coal to oil burning she became the first coastal steamer to circumnavigate Britain offering excursions at scores of places on the way. Steaming at a steady 15 knots she sailed from Glasgow to Poole in 35 hours undaunted by gales and heavy seas "After all" said David Neill "she is an ocean going ship."

Sailing on her again on her fiftieth birthday, an eighty-year old fan Donald McCulloch of Largs commented "We'll go anywhere to sail on Waverley. Stepping on this wonderful old ship makes me feel young again." "It's not just the sailing, it's a complete experience. No-one can deny any more that there is still a place for paddle steamers commented another supporter."

Captain David Neill predicted "Providing we receive the necessary support she should sail well into the twenty-first century." She has made it! Long may she continue sailing and with her long history may the good of the past cheer our present and enrich our future.

One of the things I enjoyed as a youngster helping in the business was collecting goods sent down from a Glasgow fruit market then situated in the Candle Rigs. The camaraderie of the steamer crews and the pier workers and the public was great, good humoured banter. Their common friendship while getting on with the job made trade a pleasure. I found that too when I took goods down to the steamers, vegetables, fruit and the like for ward room and dining room use. I still remember a silver-haired, fine looking wardroom steward, a Mr Mackenzie, he was courtesy and kindness and practical business combined. Caledonia MacBrayne had a man of greater worth in him than I am sure they paid. It was simply pleasure to meet him.

And that for me was Clydeside, all the way up to the birthplace of her ships. To some of us it sounded and perhaps seemed rough. Shipyard workers like miners had it rough, very rough. Battling with tough times and circumstance, little opportunity for leisure or learning in a daily struggle for survival never mind comfort can produce a rough response like a cold in the throat.

Be honest, what would you or I have been like if we had been really poor, living in a dirty street and illness a constant in the house? You might have been like the people in the Gorbals I used to see and meet. My uncle's business was there and I used to like to go with him as I did later when I was a student, just to pick up the feeling of the Gorbals and its people. I deliberately went there and round the poorest parts of Glasgow. I resented the conditions some of them had, but I liked the people. I still remember the fantastic warmth, couthieness, courage and community spirit of the old Gorbals. In my estimation most of them were great people. When razed to the ground and replaced by high flats, something of the goodness of the Gorbals disappeared.

As in war and other disasters, the community of suffering and the heart is balm and blessing not easily replaced.

Behind that, and of priceless worth, was and is the worth of our people.

The Clyde-built children of those days are very much in evidence now. Many of them are leaders in their own fields. In "The Sunday Times" 9 August 1998 is an article by Jimmy Reid entitled 'The Gang's All Here.' The gang he refers to are his friends of the fifties and sixties, all of them Clydesiders. Jimmy himself, Alec Ferguson manager of Manchester United, Billy Connolly and Gus MacDonald. If any group of men are well known and respected now – these are certainly some of them. Billy the entertainer,

Alec the fine football manager, Jimmy leader and winner of necessary strikes and last but not least Gus MacDonald.

In 1962 in Queen's Park, Glasgow the leader of the Labour Party, Hugh Gaitskell was the speaker. Listening was Donald Dewar and Gus MacDonald. Dewar, the doctor's son, and pleasant and moderate man still said that listening to Gaitskell made him go into politics. He with the late John Smith, Gordon Brown and others were the architects of the Devolution policies for Scotland. He was behind the appointment of Gus MacDonald to be the Trade and Ministry Minister at the Scottish Office. At the Gaitskell meeting, MacDonald was one of the Trotskyite hecklers who tried to drown Gaitskell out. When the call from Dewar came for his appointment to the Trade and Industry post, his biggest worry was that the government needed an answer immediately and Teen, his wife of 35 years, was at the hairdresser at Byers Road. She didn't return for two and a half hours. He was uncertain, he had just returned from holiday and had agreed to join the board of the Bank of Scotland. He had many other interests. On his wife's return she said, "Go for it." "She knew I had always been genuinely interested in Scotland's welfare, that was where my heart lay."

That was true of none more so than Donald Dewar himself. Perhaps the happiest moment of his life, was in July 1999, at the founding of the Scottish Parliament. At ease and obviously enjoying himself in the company of Her Majesty Queen Elizabeth, Donald Dewar was savouring the fulfilment of one of his life's dreams. He was appointed First Minister of the Scottish Parliament. Unfortunately for Scotland he died soon after, aged 63, of a cerebral haemorrhage on October 11th 2000.

Chapter 6

A CALLING

By the time I'd reached my "teens" I knew I was lucky. I loved life in Bute. I enjoyed Sport and I had good friends. And other members of the family did their very best for me.

My Uncle Andrew and Aunt Annie lived nearby. Most Sunday afternoons we were all invited up to their house for tea. Their family, Alex, Jean and John were there. Uncle Jack and Aunt Alice's two daughters, Jean and Alice, and myself.

The table was laden with food; a large plate of cakes at the centre. Uncle Andrew, a nice looking man and very much head of the family was very much in command, as he was in the Listers Nursery Business too. There were two things I was to remember about him. First, at the tea parties I noticed that long before the cake stage, he took his favourite cake from the pile and placed it quietly on his plate "He doesn't trust us" I thought to myself. I resolved that one day I'd beat him to it and have the nicest one first. For some reason I never did.

The next thing I long remembered was being with him in the potting shed in the Nursery. He enjoyed himself planting out the hundreds of seedlings of tomato, pansy and other plants. Together we wondered quietly at the life force of nature that makes things grow and fulfil their genetic programming. I've never lost the sense of wonder. In the more leisurely days of retirement, as we walk our dogs across the hills and through the woods and forests of Donside in Aberdeenshire I find myself amazed at the myriad of things there are great and small and all beautiful rising before our eyes. The life force and the infinite variety of it amazes me every day.

What I remember about those long ago potting-shed days was our chatting together, being interrupted by Uncle Andrew saying to me-"Ducca's a bad boy!"

I had a habit, which stayed with me, of teasing him as he worked away; with remarks such as "You've put that one in upside down" or "That wee thing'll never grow. It's half dead already." I remember my scolding him for throwing some of the plants away. "Why did you throw that one away?" I asked. "It's a weed," he replied. "But I like weeds," I'd pipe up - "They can be lovely, like flowers too!" Perhaps his chuckle and rebuke should have been more seriously made!

Nursery preparations for the great Flower Shows fascinated me. Making selections of dahlias, pansies and other floral displays and placing them in the metal holders row on row inside the large crates, took a long time. With care the crates were secured, labels clearly addressed. Then they were taken by lorries; loaded on to the Clyde Steamers at Rothesay Pier. So they went their long journeys by boat and trains to Ayr, Southport, London and other places. There they were re-assembled and shown in the Exhibitions. "Listers' Nurseries" were known then all over the country and their products sent all over the world. I longed to go to those exciting places and events. The citizens of Bute were citizens of the world.

At fourteen I wanted to get a job. In those days it was easier to get one than it is now. But my mother was determined I shouldn't join her in the business. There were no openings in the Nurseries in Barone Road, Uncle Andrew and his sons Alex and John were firmly in command. I had to go back to school what many others would have done a lot for.

But I was unsettled and lonely. And strangely troubled. I was mad about football. It was my religion. I loved it and everything about it. Like others, I dreamed of the glory of playing a great game, and being really good at it. I don't think it went much further than that. Until one night a poster about a Professional footballer caught my attention. It was announcing a meeting in a Brethren Hall in Tower Street. A player of Glasgow's Petershill Junior Football Club was speaking. I was free at night. I slipped into a back seat. I was chary about "evangelists." Those I'd seen didn't impress me at all.

Willie Graham was the name of the speaker. He was good looking, modest and had a pleasant voice. I warmed to him. He spoke simply and in a spirit of almost scientific objectivity. He would have made a good team Manager, like Craig Brown.

With hindsight I realise that, in the circumstances, he was either unusually naive or courageously honest. I can remember what he said, almost word for word.

"I never expected to speak at a meeting like this. I never had much time for the Church. I never believed Jesus of Nazareth ever thought of making a huge worldly organisation like yesterday and today's Church.

For all that I'd always been interested in who Jesus of Nazareth was and had been about. It happened so long ago, and there have been so many different ideas about what it means and what Jesus of Nazareth did and what he really said. I decided to read the Bible for myself. The Old Testament was interesting. It was the Jews Own Story. The New Testament was different and very beautiful. Do we really know what Jesus said? I honestly think that all we have are some of his words and ideas. But what wonderful words. (In today's idiom he would have said "Soundbites," "But what soundbites!") He was certainly special; really wonderful.

Two things from the story changed my ideas and my life. First, The most impossible thing; that God above loves us. Jesus said it. He was in no doubt about it. For him it was the most natural thing in life There's his words about a sparrow falling to the ground; the hairs of your head numbered, the beauty of the anemones, "the flowers of the wind." And there's the immortal stories about the lost sheep, the lost engagement ring and the lost prodigal sons. I still find it difficult to believe. But he said it!

And second, the thought that in Jesus God comes and calls us to be with Him in our lives. I couldn't get away from that. In the end I knew that that was something I couldn't get past-and I didn't want to.

Jesus says God specially loves ordinary people like you and me. He, I suppose, should know. It's his story. In a way it seems to be the point of the whole story. It's about a child born to an unmarried mother, homeless and in poverty. They were a working class family in an obscure village. The father of quite a large family was a joiner. The first born was an apprentice joiner. And the real mission of Jesus in his short life's work was to care for the poor, to heal the sick, to comfort the sad. His best friends were the "publicans and sinners," despised and rejected of society. He faced up to the leaders of Church and State. He criticised and condemned them for their lack of help and mercy to those in need. God had only one son; and he made him a carpenter who cared for people in need. He lived and died for that.

"That" he added, "is why I'm giving up professional football. I'm going out to Nigeria in Africa to try and help some of its poor people."

I was deeply moved that night. I knew and felt keenly that what every one of us, especially youngsters, need is love and a sense of belonging. I missed a real father. The message that night, and the assurance of "being loved by God in Jesus Christ" overwhelmed me. I quietly slipped out of the hall, as I had come in. "I imagine he'll help the boys of Nigeria to enjoy football and play the game perhaps for their country," I thought.

I found a sense of purpose from that night.

Some work in the spirit of that way of life, was what I decided to train for. Mr Munro, the headmaster encouraged me in forming a Scripture Union Class at school. Later I formed a Crusader Class in town. I ran it for years; and we had a great time, about forty boys coming every Sunday afternoon. At Glasgow University I joined the "I.V.F" (Inter Varsity Fellowship) - more "Christian" they said than the "S.C.M." (Student Christian Movement)! I became President and Scottish Travelling Secretary for the "I.V.F."

Inevitably I met all sorts of people. Some I liked a great deal. I was, I found, less sure of some others. The great majority were full of life and fun. I liked that.

Two individuals and incidents come to mind from that time. First George Rasmussen, George was a Dane, a great one I thought. He was a victim of rickets. You could almost pass a rugby ball through his untrousered legs. He was less than five feet tall. He was full of courage. The "Viking Spirit," I thought One night in his baker's shop he asked "Douglas, will you help me?" I would have done anything for "Wee George Rasmussen." "I want to go round the town on a Saturday night, with a Banner. Would you come with me?"

He knew I'd go with him. "When do we start?" I asked, determined not to let him down.

On one side of the banner were the words "You must be born again." That was all right. We all do. On the other side were the words "The end of the world is nigh!" I didn't much like that idea.

We went. My knees knocked a bit. The town was packed on Saturday nights with folk wanting and needing relaxation and fun. What right had I to inject religious gloom into their Saturdays. The folk knew me. I saw some nod their heads. I knew what they were thinking.

After, "declaring the end of the world," which I didn't want and Rothesay didn't deserve, I just enjoyed his company. He was a barrel of laughs, and I loved him for that. If at all possible laughter is better than weeping. If our banner carrying didn't do much good, it didn't do much harm. George married a nice girl Jess Mitchell. She was more than twice his size. I hope they had a lot of fun together.

I never knew the second man's name. I never had any desire to. The place was Keswick at the Keswick Convention. He was moderate sized. I was seventeen. He too invited me to walk with him.

As we went into the Town Square, we saw a bunch of boys, teenagers.

They had just wolf-whistled some really attractive girls who were passing them by. My accomplice took off in a spurt of fanatical religious road rage. He waded into the boys. "You're just a lot of sinners. You need to be saved etc!" The boys turned on him "We know we need to be saved, but not by you. Get lost, miserable little man!" I supported the boys, and told him so. I took myself down to Derwentwater to cool off and enjoy the beauty and peace of the lake.

A friend in those years was Tom Allan, yet to become one of the best "evangelists" Scotland ever had. He had been put off the faith by some of the "pious humbugs" as above. In France and the R.A.F. he had almost lost faith entirely. An American asked him to come with him to a service in Rheims Cathedral. At it a beautiful Negro girl sang the spiritual "Were you there when they crucified my Lord?" She sang with such simple beauty and sincerity that Tom found himself crying. The mystery and magic of Jesus Christ's total identity, with us in the forgiving love of the Cross, we with him and he with us "there" worked the miracle for Tom Allan in that hour.

I worked with him on "Seaside Missions" for children, round Scotland's coasts; and in "Tell Scotland" Missions in our cities', warehouses and shops. These were occasions of friendship, trust and pleasure with and for young and old; enjoyed and valued us such in the privilege of our common humanity. That I always felt was the sensible way to engage in mission.

But suddenly I began to rebel. I'd had enough of piety. For ever singing hymns, striving in pious prayer and comforting ourselves in holiness was not what Christianity, as Jesus had told and shown it; was about. There was more to it than that. If it was about anything, it was a this-world, down to earth affair. It was here it happened. There was Herod and his slaughter, weeping and tears as well as love and laughter.

There was a war on. It felt a just war to me and I wanted to be in it. I had to break out of unthinking loyalty to my mother. I had to be a free agent; not a kind of clone. It was time, high time, for a change.

Meeting up with other people with their different experiences and outlooks can be a help.

I'd met Tom Allan. Then I met Willie McIntyre. I realised both of them came from the Irvine Valley, a very deprived district behind Kilmarnock and both voted Labour. Willie had been Minister of the Church in Rothesay, when my mother left for the Baptists. "Why did you leave Trinity Church?" I asked my mother soon after I'd met Willie.

"Mr McIntyre preached for an hour and he preached Left Wing politics" she replied. "Would you have left if he'd preached Right Wing politics?" I teased seriously. "No, I don't think I would" she said, with a hint of a smile. "Well, I'd have been angry with him, if he hadn't preached Left-Wing politics," I said; glad that I could talk more freely to her. "He and Tom Allan were brought up in a tough area. They knew and felt the suffering and pain of poverty." She took the point and knew I was right, and that the Minister she didn't like had been right.

Next I met George Macleod. Or rather he met me. One day in a quadrangle in Glasgow University he stopped as we were passing. I'd never met him before. "Douglas" he said, as though we'd known each other for years. "Douglas, Join the Community!" Not just "How about thinking of becoming a Member of the Iona Community?" No niceties of introduction. He had his own war on. He knew I liked him and that we were on the same wavelength. I didn't join.

I'd been brought up to be a "One Nation Tory Christian!" George's slogan at the time was "Only one way - LEFT!" I wasn't ready for turning. But turning I was. George Macleod knew that. He had me from that moment and till the end of my days. Friendship with him was to be one of the greatest joys of my life.

Always I admired, and loved him. He had left St Cuthbert's Edinburgh, where he was idolised to come to Govan Old Parish Church, in the heart of Glasgow's industrial wasteland. He cared passionately for the unemployed as colleagues in need and in Christ. He formed the Iona Community to rebuild the Abbey and to rebuild the morale and body and soul of Scotland. He knew his own and Scotland's "spiritual roots were Celtic." He was in every way helping us to return to the faith of the early Celtic Church. In his presence, his handsome humanity, his magnificent voice and the beauty of his worship and works, I found myself in total agreement with him and all he was doing. The Gospel of the Carpenter had become for me the very heart of the Gospel. George Macleod's story of the stained glass window he had seen with the letter "e" missing, said it all. The words had been "Glory to God in the Highest." They now read "Glory to God in the High St.!"

On the outbreak of War I expected to be called up. Instead I was informed I was exempt from Military Duty, being in a "Reserved Occupation." I thought this was ridiculous. I'd hoped we could avoid War, but I knew Hitler's tyranny had to be stopped.

I should have joined up immediately. I waited, working away at all sorts of worthy-ish things. I used to keep a Diary regularly. I lost most of them in 1956, with all our belongings when I was arrested and imprisoned in Egypt in 1956. But I came on a small 1940 Diary the other day. I certainly was busy enough. I was keenly interested in all that was happening, not least to my friends, a friend Alfred Mylne had been fighting behind enemy lines, before the Declaration of War, and was in various campaigns. He was later captured at Tobruk. Another friend Donald Gordon engaged in scientific research was shot down and killed over the Bristol Channel. A relative Archie McKellar was honoured for valour during the Battle of Britain, one of the few. He had just been killed.

I volunteered for flying duty as a pilot. I was failed on my eyesight test. One day I found myself before the editor of the Glasgow Herald. "What can I do for you young man?" he asked.

"I want to be a War Correspondent Sir," I replied. "You need some war experience first. Join up now. Come back later." As I went out I heard his remark to his secretary. "You just sent in, Walter Mitty!" I think he was right.

I joined the O.T.C. (Officer's Training Corp) and trained with them. I was fire watching on Glasgow University tower, the night the Luftwaffe bombed Clydebank. With horror I watched poor Clydebank burn.

I offered for flying duty again and was again turned down. Having failed to become a combatant as I should have done, but having university qualifications, I volunteered for Chaplaincy duty. I was accepted. On July 4th 1945, alone, I was ordained by Dr Robert Menzies of Camphill Parish Church, Moderator of Glasgow Presbytery in Govan Parish Church.

I knew I had debts to pay. I badly wanted to try and do that. Alone, as I often seemed to be, I walked quietly out of the church through the streets of Govan. The heat hit me as I came out of the Church. Something else hit me more forcibly, the noise, the chatter, the laughter, the friendly warmth and couthiness of the folk thronging the pavements of Govan's streets. I was never ever to forget that.

I'm only glad I never did. I was always a bit on the lonely side, I needed people more, I think, than they needed me. As I stepped out of Govan Parish Church that night, I knew I was not alone. I was glad. I prayed that I might not fail them or the carpenter who had won my heart. The "common people" we read, heard Him gladly. They were and are his kind of people. They were mine too.

"CLIMB EVERY MOUNTAIN"

Climb every mountain, search high and low
Follow every by-way, every path you know.

Climb every mountain, ford every stream
Follow every rainbow till you find your dream.
Climb every mountain, ford every stream
Follow every rainbow, till you find your dream!

Chapter 6

"THE OPEN CHAMPIONSHIP"

From Germany I found myself in Carnoustie, "The Open Golf Championship" town on the east Coast of Scotland. I was to find in it the great mix of people bravely playing the game in their own way, and climbing the different ranges of mountains they encountered along the way. And I was to be impressed how magnificently they were doing it.

Never shall I forget Ben Hogan, but he was only one of many "characters" I was to meet during the next seven years in Carnoustie the East coast town at the mouth of the River Tay, and looking out to the North Sea. The Open Golf Championship played over its Links brings added attention to it worldwide. I was to discover it a place where everyone seemed to gallantly live out the town's motto "Stay the Course."

I'd just come back from Europe shattered, war-torn; all its peoples displaced-persons; disillusioned; millions of them heart-broken; hope lost; possessions gone; all mountains there ever were; to climb again; strength drained from every limb; weakness the only reality.

Carnoustie, interesting seaside, semi-industrial, golfing holiday; good farming hinterland Angus country town, was to be my first experience of a Scottish Parish. I couldn't have been more fortunate in finding a varied lot of pleasant people; each having their individual and family hills to climb.

Then and ever since I worked on the accepted parish principle "Parish (Greek paroikus = beside the house or neighbour), a manageable area to serve not to lord over or boss). This principle of very long standing Church and government and now again regaining credence as encouraging "community"; has been of immeasurable gain to Scottish and English life. In Scotland, observed and practiced nationally, it has had great and good effect on the spiritual and educational life of our people and has had much to do with the credibility of our people worldwide.

The Industrial Revolution with its build up of large cities was to make it difficult to operate; In modern form, genuine and often successful forms of "united Church" practices are being operated.

In Carnoustie in the 50's for example there was a complete mix of people of differing allegiances. Apart from the Roman Catholic priest whom I don't remember meeting all the Churches worked together. We visited and welcomed people as friends assuring them they would be most welcome. Churchgoers and non-churchgoers alike; and happy to have them if they chose to link up with any of our Churches. This spirit of co-operation in goodwill, across the board of "Church" and "Non Church" people helped enjoyable and good community.

After our experience of co-operation in Germany my family and I found particular pleasure in our Episcopal colleague, Canon Walter De Voil. A small, tubby man with a cheery face, a lovely laugh and a ready smile. It was good to know him as it is still to remember him. He dressed like a tramp, hat askew and always it seemed a long scarf several times round his neck and dangling to the ground.

One day he rang the manse bell. He was greeted by my 6 year old, Doris. She looked him up and down, appraisingly "Would you like me to go and get my mummy to give you a penny?" she said, beaming with childly concern. Walter and the rest of the town had a laugh on that for quite a while. Walter had real problems of his own. But the fun we had in sharing them, lightened loads - they lost their weight in gales of laughter.

From my earliest days in Bute, I'd had real regard for the Press; sensible and respectful co-operation, with John Mackenzie, Editor of "The Buteman"; and enjoyment of its articles, especially "By the Way" page of wayside people and events, and at the end of the paper "The Last Word" really skilful writing by a Mrs Stevenson was my introduction to really good Journalism.

In Carnoustie, we were to be lucky indeed to meet a wonderful journalist, Harry Chapman and his beautiful wife, Mina. Then and in other Parishes, I enjoyed writing news of the Churches, throwing in items that might interest the general public. Harry was the free lance reporter for the "Carnoustie Guide and Gazette" and the "Arbroath Herald." He and his wife Mina and their daughter Deirdre were to become great friends. I always was to enjoy working with reporters, but none more so than Harry Chapman.

I always found myself keen to know those who thought and felt differently from the so-called orthodox line. I'd always felt a bit different myself; somehow odd-man-out; and I felt on the same wavelength of the "unorthodox."

In Carnoustie I became very friendly with the one Communist in town, John Brown. After a long and tiring day I used to drop in to have a chat and a cup of tea with Mr and Mrs Brown. John simply felt as most of the

Communists of that time did that we must create a better society and he didn't think the Church came out well on that front. I always enjoyed a good argument with him. Later I felt slightly sorry for him; his two daughters Ann and Meg joined a First Communicants class. Then they told me they had not been baptised. I suggested a short service after church, but they wanted to be baptised in the face of the congregation. They were. I told John. He was really quite pleased.

But it was Ben Hogan I was to remember most dramatically. Hogan had been involved in a serious car accident with crippling injuries. He came out of it just alive, with his golfing future and career almost certainly ended. There was never very much of him, but what there was - fighter and survivor. A never say die material. He came back. He was in the field of competitors on the links in the Open Golf Championship of this great year at Carnoustie 1953.

I was a "steward." I remember a slim, thin figure in the distance on the tee. Thousands of spectators stood in respectful silence as becomes those who know the hazards, nuances and endless impossibilities of ordaining the ultimate destiny of a tiny ball at the impulsive mercy or impatience of an unpredictable person; of millions of strained nerves and twitching muscles and the awesome crises of every club's contact with a golf ball quietened by that and recognition of the "great's" insignificant but important stance at a tee.

The fairway between Hogan and me was the narrowest of ways, in the awesome silence I heard the click of a ball being clearly hit. With the crowds I looked to the skies. I saw it, the ball, flying high against the blue sky. On it came, on and on and on, perfectly, infallibly. It dropped with a plop on the green. The crowd roared. I stood deep in the grass in disbelief, complete unbelief rather. Impossible, perfection. I have never been so impressed in my life. This little man there, cool, modest perfectionist. Once given up for dead and finished he went on to do the same till the end of the round and win the championship. There has never for me been anyone better than Hogan.

Carnoustie was to leave me forever with the precious memory of fine people, facing up to the challenge of their own kind of mountains; and tackling them with great spirit.

The mountains were there; for the climbing. And they did.

1953 was to be that kind of year, in a special and memorable way. Her Majesty the Queen was crowned; and her crowning coincided with the first conquest of Everest by Edmund Hillary and Sherpa Tenzing. In those conquests of land, sea and air our British conquerors are normally remembered. They are our heroes; and they deserve to be honoured.

People like the Ghurkas, the Sikhs and Sherpas tend to be forgotten. I still take off my hat to Sherpa Tenzing and others like him who have helped our heroes to win their honours. The leader of the expedition Brigadier John Hunt published his story in "The Ascent of Everest": Hunt says "Tenzing was specially delighted to be given the privilege with Hillary of doing the last bit of the climb. All through our work of stock piling he had necessarily undertaken the least exciting tasks of all, leading the low level ferries or organising ration and firewood parties sending and receiving mail runners at base and helping to keep all his men cheerful. These things he had done well and willingly for it was his nature to do so, but I knew his heart was set on getting higher and higher still, always he was happiest when climbing. Now he was to have a chance to show his mettle and show it he did. This man who did the humble dull thing when his heart was on the heights. So they climbed and at the end Hillary and Tenzing grappled with suicidally dangerous stretches of climbing and then 29,000ft up a few more whacks of the ice axe and they stood on top."

My seven years in my first Parish was to give me experience of many men, women and young people who were happiest when climbing their particular mountains. I was happy with them, and proud of them.

Chapter 8

EGYPTIAN DIARY – 1956

We were very happy in Carnoustie and not thinking of moving until I was approached about becoming Chaplain to "The Suez Contractors Limited" operating in the Canal Zone of Egypt. Through the years the Church of Scotland had accepted requests for Scots abroad to have their own Minister. As a result congregations of the Church of Scotland had been formed round the world. This part of the Church's work in the fifties was for long under the wise and capable leadership of Dr Alexander King ably assisted by his Secretary Miss May Slidders. Together, they ran what was then known as "The Colonial and Continental" Committee of the Church. Its work was the supervision of congregations across Europe, in Gibraltar, Lisbon, Paris, Vienna, Rotterdam, Amsterdam, Genoa, Rome; in the Middle East Jerusalem, Cairo. In South America, congregations in Chile, Rio de Janeiro and in Central America and the West Indies Havana, Trinidad and Tobago and in Africa and the East-Nairobi, Mombasa, Bombay, Madras, Kalimpong, Assam, Calcutta, Colombo in Ceylon. Dr. King and Miss Slidders treated the Ministers in those places and their congregations as members of the family and they succeeded in making them feel just that. It was to all intents and purposes a real Bishopric within the Church of Scotland, and there couldn't have been a better one.

From time to time, new situations arose where the appointment of a Minister was requested. The retreat of Britain from Egypt in 1955 was one such. A clause in the agreement with the Egyptian Government allowed for Britain to remain in the important Canal Zone for six years; time in which to run down the large Ammunition, Maintenance, Electrical and Engineering Depots in the region. Two thousand Staff and family personnel had to be stationed in Moascar Ismailia, Fayid by the Great Bitter Lake, and Tel-el Kebir in the Desert; with all the community requirements to create a settled community.

"The Suez Contractors Ltd" was the name of the Company established by the Government to do that.

I was asked to volunteer. After considerable delay I did.

I found leaving Carnoustie rather a wrench. Only Marion's desire for the sunshine, and mine for adventure decided the issue.

Farewells said, I flew out to my new job. I didn't know what to expect. I was prepared to see out my six year Contract.

I flew out from Blackbushe on Friday 13th January 1956. I was arrested at midnight on Halloween night 31st October 1956, and imprisoned, with my congregation in Cairo, until our release when the last of the British and French soldiers left Egyptian soil. President Nasser of Egypt, angered by America renaging on its promise of aid for him in building the Aswan Dam, nationalised the Suez Canal on 26th July. That effectively put paid to our six year Contracts. The British Government made a great political issue of the matter. The Contractors families were ordered home to Britain; and after months of uncertainty, on the last weekend of October, Britain, Israel and France attacked and invaded Egypt. On the 31st October, we the Contractors, were arrested at gunpoint and imprisoned in Cairo.

I had all our belongings packed and ready to take with me; two cases. All I was able to take with me was a Diary concealed in my pocket.

As we queued to enter the Abdine Palace in Cairo on the 1st of November as prisoners of the Egyptian government I had my diary in my hand. I saw the Egyptian guard was looking at it. As I passed into prison he asked "Is that a Bible you have in your hand?" That took me a bit by surprise. I heard myself say "Yes" not altogether untruthfully. It was my "Diary 1956." "Bible" ("Biblia") "means "books!" The Egyptian Guard confessed to me that he was a Coptic Christian!

The following excerpts from the Diary may help to paint the picture of the eventful year 1956,"The Year of Suez," which virtually decided the end of the British Empire.

Friday January 13th

As I step out of the plane the heat of the desert blasts my face. Bernard Smith Secretary of the Contractors greets me. As we motor to Moascar, Ismailia, a liner sails across the desert; its red funnel and upper decks aloft. Then the Suez Canal comes into view, quite impressive. By the desert road fellahine are busy; water drawn my simple round mills helps them grow large water melons, cabbages, courgettes, tomatoes and lettuce, fruits and flowers.

Saturday January 14th

We are billeted in the Zikkri Hotel, Moascsar until housing can be arranged. The Contractors are housed in three compounds used by the army; Kensington Village, Fayid near the Great Bitter Lake (I have to go there);

Moascar itself and Tel El Kebir in the desert. From the hotel's flat roof there's a good view of the town. I enjoy the plaintiff sound of donkeys braying. Are they indulging in some kind of donkey gossip or complaining about their lot? We are told not to go into the native quarters, a sensible enough order. But that's what I always like to do; and do. Seeing the people and life as it is; keeping watch as I go but enjoying, "soaking up" the reality of things as they really are.

January 18th

I go to Cairo to see Bishop Frank Johnston (a Scot) who will be boss of the Anglican Chaplain Michael Powell due out in six weeks. I suggest and he readily agrees we work on a "combined operations" basis. Frank Johnston entirely agrees and is glad that is how I feel.

Sunday February 19th

United service in Moascar for the licensing of Michael Powell, Bishop Johnston officiates. Michael and his wife seem very nice.

Saturday March 3rd

Jordan dismisses Glubb Pasha as leader of the Arab Legion.

Sunday March 11th

The Very Rev. G. D. Henderson Moderator of the General Assembly on a tour of European and Middle Eastern Churches visits us to install me officially and ordain my new Kirk Session of Church of Scotland, Methodist, Baptist and Church of Ireland men.

Monday March 12th

To Cairo where we sign President Nasser's book and take in the Pyramids and Sphinx. Lunch at Bishop Johnston's house. General Manager John Foden and Sir Humphrey, British Ambassador, and Lady Trevelyan among the guests. All we need is President Nasser.

Friday 16th March

Marion, Pauline, Doris and David fly out to Abu Sueir. Pauline unhappy about having to fly on her birthday. Great to have them out.

Thursday 29th March

Nasser in "Observer" interview indicates he has lost confidence in Britain and in the United Nations and emphasises the independence of the Arab world.

Sunday 29th April

Congregations are building up splendidly. Canal pilots Dick Henderson and Derek Mavitty are super. To Derek and Marjory Mavitty for lunch. Derek goes off to take the ship "Sterling Victory" up the Canal.

Saturday 9th June

Preparations for the Liberation Festivities triumphant arches going up all over the place. One can't but understand the reason for their pleasure and yet it is rather sad that it should be our going that gives them such delight.

Friday 22nd June

Phone call at 6 a.m. from Bob Montgomery saying that Isobel Shankland had lost her baby. Ian, her husband, wants me to go up to Cairo with him. I do so and spend all day with them. Ian and Isobel from Paisley a really nice young couple.

Pathetic thing to have to lower the small coffin of a child all ready to live and not given the opportunity. In this case a perfectly formed lovely little chap. It seems the birth itself was too much for the wee fellow to survive. Odd indeed.

Sunday 24th June

Been busy preparing the K. V. Courier which goes to all houses and get to bed at 2 a.m. It has been quite a hard week. Rise at 6 a.m. to go to "Tek" where another good gathering. I enjoy being with them and taking the service.

Tuesday 26th June

Read a book on "Pharaoh to Farouk" and knock together an article for the "Courier" - "Egyptian Backcloth" honest but thought provoking.

Wednesday 18th July

Phone call from Bernard Smith in which he informs me he has to vet the K.V. Courier before it goes out. It appears the English leadership does not like the truth, if it is honest, critical and supportive in any way of an "occupied people" (being on the management committee I answer this forcefully on the basis "sack me if you will" as you did Father Hodges, but Ministers of the Church of Scotland are not easily gagged and what I wrote was quite simply the truth). Father Hodges a convert from Protestantism had been sent home for criticising the manager's wife who had married a Protestant. While dancing with me one night the Manager's wife had said "Father Hodges won't grant me absolution." "Well perhaps the Lord will" I replied.

43

Friday 27th July

In speech in Alexandria last night Nasser nationalised the Canal in order to finance the Aswan Dam. Foster Dulles American Foreign Secretary had promised substantial aid, but withdrawn the offer in view of the American election and Jewish lobby pressure. The French "hand over" of the Canal has four years to run. Has Nasser's enthusiasm and youth led him beyond the bounds of wisdom or not? I cannot help sympathising with him on many counts, not least our and the French's broken promises to our colonies including Egypt. The family is greatly enjoying things here.

Saturday 4th August

Marion and I are confident the trouble will settle and blow over. Time alone will tell. At any rate we do not want to separate and do not have the money to finance a return voyage!

Sunday 5th August

Morning Service at Fayid. Good choir and congregation. Along the Canal which is beautiful and peaceful for Service at Moascar. Down to Dick and Maud Henderson, after Service for lunch. Discover Maud is ready to take off, with the family, for home, having been through similar trouble before, she is not keen on another dose. This looks like being rather an upset for the pilots before much longer, enjoy being with the Hendersons; then motor into the desert for evening service at Tel-el-Kebir, which turns out to be small but select. I'll always remember the egrets reflected in all their beauty in the still waters of the desert canals. Theirs seems to be the peace we lack.

Home late after a full and busy day away from Marion and the family. A pity but there it is.

Monday 6th August

News seeps through that "Evacuation" of wives and children is compulsory. A London Government order. Not knowing much about it all, I take Marion and the family down to the Club for a rest. We may not be together for much longer. We have a swim in the cool waters of Lake Timsah, which is nice. I meet Steve, who indicates the terms of the families return home, may be reasonable. It seems sensible to accept the inevitable. Exactly how soon the families may have to leave we don't yet know.

In the evening as arranged, Mr. Wyatt, who is on his own and I think lonely, comes in with some Gilbert and Sullivan music. We play back some of ours, which we hadn't touched since I'd brought them out. I like Jimmy Shand and his Band best.

I see in the Diary at this point "Prayers I used in the service last night": "Watch Thou dear Lord with those who wake and give Thine angels charge over those who sleep. Tend Thy sick ones O Lord Christ, rest Thy weary ones Bless Thy dying ones Soothe Thy suffering ones Shield and perfect Thy joyous ones. Be present O merciful Lord and protect us through the silent hours of this night so that wearied though we are by the chances and changes of this fleeting world we may repose on Thine eternal changeless-ness trusting in Thy everlasting mercy so we will lay us down in peace and take our rest."

Thursday 9th August

Marion, attractive as ever and my rather lovely little family of three leave the quay at Port Said for the voyage home on the Boschfontein of the Netherlands Africa Line. The ship I'm afraid is packed to the gunnels (from then on the Contractors was a "men only" affair all hoping for a settlement of what was basically a British, French Israel plot and a tedious charge and counter charge affair, Egypt obviously the victim.

Sunday 21st October

Invited to take part in the 21st Anniversary Service of the Battle of El Alamein at the cemetery site on this date. I organised a party to go. Forty of us go via Alexandria spend a night and motor along the Mediterranean coast through silvery sand and fig plantations the view of the sea is very lovely. El Alamein cemetery set in the middle of the desert is impressive in its simplicity. The service has the same characteristic simplicity. Bishop Johnston preaches, Parry conducts, British Ambassador Sir Humphrey Trevelyan reads the lesson, I take the prayers. Representatives of the British Legion the Services, Ambassadors of all Commonwealth countries and Major General Ahmed Salem representing President Nasser attend.

Apart from the great Crusader Sword noble against the clear blue sky the 12,000 white crosses in the ground and 8,000 names inscribed on the memorial around us. In the peace and beauty of the day it was difficult to realise how important battles these deserts knew. Only the merest fraction of the real cost and loss was before our remembering eyes.

Monday 28th October

I plant out my garden with zinnias, sweet peas, frangi panis and other plants - in hope, and on a lovely day. The question "Will they live or die; and will we live to see them?"

Tuesday 29th October

Aly my suffragi shakes me about 7 a.m. "What is it Ali?" I ask. "Wake up! The Israelis are on the other side of the Canal. They are invading Egypt. They have come 100 miles through our Sinai Desert. They wouldn't have found it difficult to get to the Canal." So this is what has been happening in the eerie quiet of the last week.

Wednesday 30th October

Ali and I listen to a speech on the radio by Anthony Eden "Unless Israel withdraws 10 miles east of the Suez Canal (i.e. 90 miles inside Egypt) and Egypt withdraws 10 miles west of the Canal (i.e. 110 miles behind her own borders, leaving her own cities her own Canal life line defenceless and open to the invader) British and French airforces will bomb and troops will occupy the Canal zone!!" Ali listens and says "Eden is stupid." "No," I can only reply "Not stupid, quite, quite wrong and mad. "The Empire is back at its worst."

Thursday 31st October

It looks like the end of the line. What's the hell. Two of the boys are having a birthday party. I go and enjoy myself with the rest. We enjoyed the first half of our Halloween Party. About midnight, on my way back to the house, an Egyptian Army Sergeant armed to the teeth, emerged out of the darkness. "Halt" he hollers "Who goes there?" (Where did he learn that?) "Ana Assis" "O I am a Priest" I replied confidently and cheerfully. I've always been an ass I think. I think I was suffering from slightly too much spiritual inspiration in addition. "I am going to 'The Manse' now perhaps Hell later; but I hope not soon." He was a fat chap; and marched me home. "Stay there till I come back. I'll arrest some more prisoners. He did and threw them in to 'The Manse'- one in his pyjamas, another without his false teeth; all of them distinctly bolshie and fed up. I read a book and tried to soften up the Sergeant with friendly conversation. I had a big bar of Cadbury's Dairy Milk Chocolate, of which I offered him some. At first he declined. After a while of my cursing Eden, praising Nasser and Allah too, he accepted and greatly enjoyed several pieces of chocolate; and relaxed enough to imitate something like a smile.

We had taken to Egypt most of the things we treasured; Marion's jewellery and dresses, ornaments, diaries, photographs, books, music and last, and least important perhaps, all my Sermons. I had everything packed in two cases. The Sergeant, liar that he was, assured us we'd get back to our houses in an hour or two, after investigation up the road. Of course, we never did. We waited in the Community Centres all night.

1st November

In the early hours of the morning we were taken by buses to Cairo, and lined up in the Square by the Abdine Palace. Crowds gathered, swore and spat at us and pelted the buses with stones. As we were marched inside the Prison Guard noticed the Diary I had in my jacket. He turned out to be a "Coptic Christian." We were questioned, passed through and imprisoned in the "El Khedewiyya Concentration Camp" it said on the gates was we were driven in. I was one of 18 in a room. It wasn't comfortable; air raid sirens kept sounding; it was in the poorer Arab quarter. Outside was a lot of noise and a lot of hysterical people.

We didn't have anything to drink for ten days and food was minimal we survived. Things got better when a representative of the Swiss government was allowed in as mediator. I had been arrested only wearing an old suit and looked pretty awful, but I contacted the commandant, a nice chap. He took my word for it that I was a padre and allowed me freedom to visit all floors of the prison. One of the boys had smuggled in a radio. Cyprus radio gave us the news of the outside world. I gathered empty cigarette cartons; wrote out the news on them and dropped them to all the rooms each day. So we knew what was going on. After ten days or so the Commandant gave us permission to get outside in the morning for an hour. I was able to carry on with my job and had all sorts of conversations with all sorts of different types of men. We got on fine. One Saturday morning, at breakfast, as I bit into a very hard roll, I heard an ominous crack. My dental plate had gone. I tried to cancel the Sunday Service; but there was something of a riot. "Please take the Service, Padre" the hypocrites cried. I whistled my way through it. The sermon was on the words to Moses - the Union Rebel leader in Egypt. "I know your sorrows and am come down to deliver you." The spiritual content was lost on the gang. They got the other bit quite well! I never heard more powerfully pious singing Hymns like "God bless and pity us, Shine on us with thy grace" and "Fight the Good Fight."

The Lord's Prayer was spat out; and the Amens thundered from the throats of the most fervid and holy of the Saints. It was a good service. But I was glad to get my plate back on Monday and repaired for nothing. Things were looking up.

Saturday 24th November

Frank Terry from Aylesbury in our room sings and writes poetry and stutters, but in the loo I notice he doesn't stutter. I wondered why. The stutter was a blind. He was a spy and he was rather frightened. Next day he shaved off his beard. He came to me and said, "Here is a new hymn I would like sung to the tune of the old hundredth." I agreed only to discover what it was "We'll sing it at Morning Service outside tomorrow" said Frank it wasn't the best of poetry. I was quite moved by it. "All right" I said. He had written out copies of it on odd bits of paper and cigarette carton backs, to the tune the Old 100th.

Sunday 25th November

Our special "Freedom Day" as it turned out to be. The men had a good chuckle together as they sang Frank Terry's hymn in the sunshine of a morning, when we first felt we might soon be free. In fact we had quite a time to wait in uncertain hope. Our Hymn Sheet a la Frank Terry read:-

"Dedicated to the Rev. Douglas Lister, for the wealth of friendship and faith he offered us during internment in Egypt.

> *"The Lord our God has made it clear*
> *That we should all be free*
> *For life is freedom without fear*
> *With love eternally*
>
> *We bend our hearts today to Him*
> *That He may see our plight*
> *And offer to Him prayer, and sing*
> *The praises of His might*
>
> *The mighty power that gives us life*
> *Be with us ever more*
> *We know that others seek His hand*
> *We know His strength will fight all strife*

His love is ever sure
Their prayers and needs are ours
And with His strength they'll firmly stand
The pain of present hours.

The Lord our God is good indeed
He gives us life and health
He tends us, guides us, heeds our needs
And all His love is wealth.

The Lord our God is ever near
And we shall soon be free
Our path to freedom now is near
We praise Him thankfully."

Frances Joseph Terry
24th Nov. 1956

We were allowed up to the flat roof for an hour 3.15 - 4.15 p.m. To the S.W. we can see Maadi village and the Pyramids. To the south the masts of falookahs on the Nile, to the north the citadel and Mohammed Ali mosque, to the east the Makkottam Hills. The passages and rooms of the prison ring with the whistling and singing of "Scotland the Brave," the theme song of the Voice of Freedom Station evidently being broadcast in Scotland on a BBC wavelength. This news heard this morning brightens our day adding its touch of humour and causing talk of internment in the Tower when we touch down. In the afternoon hour on the roof the singing of virtually a massed choir of Free Scotland singers impresses all the guards who feel a kindred spirit with us and for us. The sound and lively spirit of the contractors carried I was told well into Cairo.

Tuesday 18th, Wednesday 19th and Thursday 20th December
We are told to prepare to leave. There are several false starts.

Thursday 20th December
I finish reading John Buchan's "Midwinter." "Alistair MacLean" he writes, "had lost tragically yet found there was more to prize than he had dreamed." A significant way to end?

Friday 21th December

We leave and go by train via Ismailia to Kantara where UNO Indian guards take over. We pass Egyptian prisoners of the invasion. They shout "Hail Nasser" and swear and spit viciously at us. As the train trundles on to the Abbas Quay at Port Said we are met by troops of the Royal Scots who give us a drink of "Auld Kirk." How sweet it is as is the air of freedom. We have lost everything, but we have our lives and our freedom. We board the S.S. Asturias en route for Cyprus. In the morning a very large congregation gathers for our farewell service. I preach on Acts chapter 28 "He thanked God and took courage." We flew home in old orange crates, but they stayed air-borne!

Nothing was ever recorded of the Contractors' experience in the British Press, Radio or Television.

Roy Plomley's B.B.C. Radio Programme "Desert Island Discs" was based on the choice of music individuals might like to hear if, like Robinson Crusoe" they were stranded on a Desert Island. The programme is still running although Mr. Plomley has died.

The real Robinson Crusoe belonged to Largo in Fife. The following chapters are based on Largo.

Chapter 9

TWO SAILORS OF LARGO

The one will live for ever, the other is remembered as just a sailor. They are Robinson Crusoe and Sir Andrew Wood.

Robinson Crusoe grew up in the small fishing village of Lower Largo in the attractive East Neuk of Fife. King James VI of Scotland and 1st of England described the Kingdom of Fife as "a beggar's mantle fringed with gold." The "fringe of gold" is that part of Fife that stretches with mile on mile of golden beaches from Largo to the home of golf, St. Andrews.

"Robinson Crusoe," the delight of children and adult children is the story Daniel Defoe made of the real life adventures of Alexander Selcraig or Selkirk.

He was born in 1676, the seventh son of John, a tanner and leather worker in the seatown of Largo.

A clever boy was young Alex., good at mathematics and navigation at school but wild; and one of a roughish family. The old Kirk Session records tell the story, On 25th Aug. 1695 Alexr. was summoned for "undecent beavier in ye church." Unseemly laughter at ye Minister! On 27th Aug, "ye session mett." It was noted "Alex" Selcraige did not compear, being gone away to ye seas; this business is continued till his return." Then six years later the record tells of a good going family row in the father's house. In November 1701 we find "delated" John Selcraige, elder and his wife Euphan Mackie and Alexander and Andrew Selcraig for disagreement together and John Selcraige and his wife Margaret Bell. All of them are ordered to be cited agst, the next session which is to be the 25th of this instant."

On the 25th Novr. we find John Selcraige being "examined what was the occasion of the tumult that was in his house. He said he knew not but in the house," his brother Andrew Selcraige haiving brought in a canefull of salt water, of which his brother Alexander did drink, through mistake, and he laughing at him for it, his brother Alexr "came and beat him." Upon which he rune out of the house and called his brother John. John testified that "as he came in the door he did see his brother Alexr, in the other end of the house casting off his coat and coming towards him, where upon his father did get betwixt them. He knew not what he did other ways, his head being borne down by his brother Alexr, but afterwards being liberated by his wife did make his escape." Margaret Bell said "that she did follow her husband and coming into the house she found Alex. Selcraige gripping both her father and her husband, and she labouring to loose Alexander's hands from her husbands head and breast her husband fled out of doors and she followed him and called back again "You fals loon will you murder your father and my husband both". Whereupon he followed her to the door but wither he beat her or not she was in so great confusion she cannot distinctly tell but ever since she hath a sore pain in her head. "Alexander was called but "compeared not because he was at Cupar, he is to be cited pro secundo agst. the next session."

When the session next met on the 29th Nov," After prayer Alexr. Selcraige scandalous for contention and disagreeing with his brother was called and compeared and being questioned" he confessed to the tumult and beating his brother Andrew twice with a strafe." He confessed also that "he challenged his eldest brother John to a combate as he called it of "drynieffels," which he did afterwards repent and regrate." On Nov. 30 Alexander Selcraige, according to the session's appointment compeared before the pulpit and made acknowledgment of his sin in disagreeing with his brother and was rebuked in the face of the congregatison for it,and promised amendment in the strength of the Lord,and so was dismissed."

Shortly after this he took the opportunity of a voyage to London,where we find him joining the celebrated William Dampier in a privateering voyage to the South Seas in the ships "St. George" and the "Cinque Ports." Selcraige "born to the seas" had voyaged before. Dampier appointed him "Sailing Master" of the "Cinque Ports."

It was on this voyage that Selkirk quarrelled with his Captain Stradling. The punishment Selcraige got for his insubordination was to be sent ashore, marooned on Juan Fernandez where he remained for four years and four months before being taken off by Capt. Woodes Rogers. His story got widespread publicity and Daniel Defoe brought immortality to his adventures in "Robinson Crusoe." Selcraige returned to Largo but became something of a recluse, longing for his island.

Naturally enough, perhaps a statue to his memory was erected in Lower Largo, on the site of the house where he was born.

The other sailor, contributed more to the cause of Scotland's national honour, but is not so well known, Sir Andrew Wood. Born about the middle of the 15th Century in a thatched cottage "under the shadow of the church on the knoll" in Upper Largo, where a Church had stood for many centuries, Andrew Wood too was a gifted boy.

In a rather different way from Selkirk. Selkirk and all of Largo would have heard of the exploits of his fellow villager of the previous century, "Sir Andrew Wood of Largo, the great Scottish Admiral" Young Andrew Wood of Upper Largo after school years at the village school sailed across the River Forth in the Ferry to Edinburgh and the Port of Leith, and its busy trade.

These were stirring times both at home and abroad. News of world events "furth of Scotland" came from the South by the ships and stage-coaches moving constantly to and fro. News of the Inca and Aztec conquests; news of Vasco da Gama's and Ferdinand Magellan's voyages round the South of Africa and southernmost tip of South America and later of Christopher Columbus's discovery of the Americas. And more relative to Wood and Scotland news of the French successes against England on the Continent at the ending of the Hundred Years War. This, in a real sense is where Andrew Wood of Largo was to come into his own. For Scotland favoured France, as part of the "auld alliance" as against "England," the "auld enemy."

Wood's outstanding gifts of personality and success as a merchant trader brought him public attention notoriety and recognition.

After Bannockburn, Robert the Bruce had seen the point of having some "men of war" to serve Scotland's cause, and he gave attention to ship-building at Cardross. but it was in the reigns of James III and James IVth, the 15th and 16th centuries, that anything like a "Scottish Navy" developed. James III was the first king after Bruce to appreciate sea power, and he built quite an efficient fleet. The ships he built and purchased served the dual role of merchantmen in peace and fighting ships in war. So it came about that the merchant skippers of Leith, then Lothians and Fife were for many years the country's bulwarks against Scandinavian, French, Flemish, Spanish and English warships and privateers.

Into this national need Wood fitted perfectly. He had first been merely a merchant skipper who fought his own way at sea, but he had done so with great success. He had frequently taken on and defeated the ships of Edward IV of England and Alfonso, King of Portugal, and privateers of other nations. James III sought out Wood and appointed him Admiral of his fleet He knighted him on the deck of his own ship "The Yellow Frigate" in 1482 and bestowed on him the lands and barony of Largo,which he held by the tenure that he should at all times be ready to pilot and convey the King and Queen to the shrine of St. Adrian, on the Isle of May. Wood had a Castle built at Largo, made for him by some of the English, French and Portuguese pirates he had captured at sea. They won their liberty by fulfiling their contract to build the Castle.

Treachery and intrigue were at work in the nation at the time. The King was popular with the people. The nobility did not approve and were for an alliance with England. Plots were afoot to marry off Margaret Tudor, Henry VII's daughter to James, the Duke of Rothesay the King's son. Wood had the confidence of the King and friendship with his son. When the King, James III was murdered at Sauchieburn, Wood remained a constant source of encouragement to his son, James, now James IVth.

Here again,Wood came into his own. Successful resistance to English incursion and threatened invasion, played a great part in creating the legend of "Sir Andrew, the great Scottish Admiral" The English Captain Howard in his good ship "Harry" led plunder raids round the Scottish Coast. Wood, for his part, with his fleet of ships, including the "Yellow Caravel" or "Frigate" was always on the watch to intercept the enemy.

The "Caravel" carried a crew of 500 and 50 guns firing forty eight pounders, and that of his Second Command, Mathieson had a substantial crew and 20 guns. They were not to be treated lightly. The whole of Fife and most of Scotland knew of them and supported them. "The Fleet" of the 16th Century in Scotland had the same emotive connotation that it had in the 20th Century. "The Fleet's In" raised the same sense of euphoria and pride then as in our modern times.

A fierce battle off Dunbar had resulted in a thrashing of the English by Wood, with the capture of five of their ships. Henry VII the King of England refused to take this slap in the face lying down. He refurbished his navy in 1488 and sent three ships under the command of Sir Stephen Bull, to humiliate Wood and bring Scotland to heel. They intercepted Wood on a

"The Yellow Frigate"

return from a trading mission to Holland, and a bloody battle ensued off Largo Bay and Fifeness. Wood in "The Yellow Frigate" and Mathieson in "The Flower" took on the three English ships and there was much loss of life in the infighting that developed when the ships grappled with one another. Great crowds on the Fife shore watched the fighting off the coast. In the end the English ships surrendered and were brought into Dundee; their navy's defeat complete.

Wood continued to serve his country, but his favourite retreat was to his castle two hundred yards to the West of the Church, overlooking Largo Bay and the scenes of his greatest victories. With the oncoming of age he had a canal dug from his castle to the Church. And each Sunday he had some of his English prisoners of war still in his service row him in the barge to "Mass."

His friendship with and support of the good King James IVth was total. But it was to turn to tragedy when in 1513, the King James IVth was killed, and a third of Scotland's best leaders and men, at the Battle of Flodden. Wood was broken hearted, and spent his last years in sorrow at Scotland's great loss. When he died at a ripe old age, he was borne in his barge by torchlight down the Canal to his last resting place in the vault of Largo Church. A simple memorial slab marks the grave of one of Scotland's most gallant sailors.

A member and friend of Largo Kirk, Mr. Dan Marshall made me a Model of Sir Andrew Wood's Ship, "The Yellow Frigate." It hangs in Largo Kirk in honour of a brave man.

Chapter 10

"CHRISSIE"

Raven-haired, an open welcoming manner and a laugh that shattered the sabbath quiet of the village-that was Chrissie. She seemed Scottish enough. She regularly visited her aunt, gracious Miss Cameron, who lived in the cottage just in front of the Manse in Upper Largo. Chrissie Cameron was her own name. We often met,our meetings were usually accompanied by friendly laughter. There was something different about her. One day I asked her about her roots. "Do you have any Spanish blood in your veins?" I asked. To gales of explosive laughing, Chrissie, said "How amazing, how did you know?" "Yes, I do" she remarked, "I came in with the wreck of the Spanish Armada at Ainster. (Anstruther) when Mr. James Melville was Minister there."

The night before at St. Andrew's Presbytery I had moved that "James Melville's Manse" should be preserved in use and redecorated. James Melville (1556-1614) was an impressive personality.

The Manse that he had built for him by some of his tradesmen parishioners, was built in the record time of six months, "with never a soar finger during the haill labour." He had oversight of most things in the fishing burgh. He had the Manse made, to stand sentinel over the whole surrounding land and sea-scape; to enable him to see and know all that was going on,in the interests of order and peace. Three hundred years after, James Melville's Manse stands guard over this lovely "East Neuk" town.

Soon after I came nearer to finding Chrissie's forefathers; a booklet told the story. "A St. Andrew's Diarist - James Melville 1556-1614 - The Dow Lecture - 14th October 1963" by Sir William Arbuckle.

These were stirring times on the political and religious fronts. The return of James Melville's powerful and aggressive Uncle, Andrew Melville, was to stir up things more than most. His determination was that Presbyterianism, not Roman Catholicism or Episcopacy should rule in Scotland. He drove a hard bargain, not least with the King, King James VIth of Scotland and 1st of England. At Falkland Palace, Melville, "small and light of body though he was," berated the King, calling him but "God's sillie vassal," and "taking him "be the slieve" demanded it the duty of a Christian King to be guided by the Church of Christ, "whose subject King James the

Saxt is, and of whose kingdome nocht a king, nor a lord, nor a heid, bot a member" Andrew Melville was lucky that James the king "dsimitted us pleasantlie."

His nephew, James Melville of Anstruther was of kindlier, more humane mettle.It was through his tolerant, amenable disposition that Chrissie Cameron came to grace the "kingdom of Fife!" In his first year as Minister there, he was upset by happenings at the harbour. An English pirate ship plundered an Anstruther boat, killed one of the crew; went on to Pittenweem to attack another vessel lying there.

The men of Anstruther fitted out a fast vessel, and with a strong boat of St.Andrew's went in search of the Englishman; tracked it down to the Suffolk coast, drove it aground and captured the crew.

Returning to Anstruther the men brought news of the Spaniards invasion of England," the Armada of Spain were coming,"

> They came to Anstruther a year later–1589. "Earlie in the morning," wrote Melville, "be brak of day, ane of our bailyies cam to my bedsyde, saying (but nocht with fray) "I haiff to tell yow newes "Ther is arryvit within our berbried this morning a schipe full of Spainyarts, bot nocht to giff mercie bot to ask." Therfor desyrit me to ryse and hair thair petition with tham. Upse I got with diligence, and assembling the honest men of the town, came to the Tolbuthe. The Captain, twitching my scho with his hand, began his harang in the Spanise toung, wharof I understud the substance, and being about to answer in Latine, he haiffing onlie a youing man with him to be his interpreter, began to us in guid Einglis.

In the end Melville, told the Spanish Officers and men, that, although they were the King's enemies," and they were frinds to the graiest enemie of Christ, the Pape of Rome, and were attacking our neighbour Eingland; "we war men, sa moved be human compassion, and Christiannes of a better relligion nor they, they souldn find na thing amangs us bot Christian pitie and warks of mercie and almes..." And efter the sam speitches we receivved them in our hous, intertained tham humeanlie, sufferit the souldiours to com a-land, to the humber of threttin score, in the maist part yoiung, berdles men, sillie, trauchled and houngered."

The Spainyarts were thuis given halesome parritdge and cabbages and being well fed were happy."

There were those who accauseds James Melville and the Baillies of Anstruther of traitrous "beavier." But Melville resisted all criticism and was left alone.

Having met and always having enjoyed the good and amusing company of Chrissie Cameron of Upper Largo, I'm glad things worked out that way in Anstruther in 1589.

"The Captaine, a man of big stature,and grave and stout countenance, grey-heared, and verie humble lyk, with his face neir the ground "was received with mercie by us!"

Chapter 11

THE HAT LADIES OF LUNDIN LINKS

In my time there, Leven Road, Lundin Links was full of characters: the Steels, the Rogers, the Lings, the Burgesses, the Shepherds and the Edwards. There was none quite to compare with the hat ladies of Lundin Links. None was more interesting to me than Miss Annie S Telfer and her sister. She always seemed to walk a step ahead of her sister, her silent shadow. They had run a milliner's business in Kirkcaldy. When we saw two highly decorated bird's nest like hats walking behind a wall we knew it was the Telfer sisters on the march. Annie, squat like, moved slowly and surely like an intelligent and reasonable kind of little feminine tank, but certainly a tank.

She had about her, what I'd always wanted and lacked, the quiet certainty that she was right. I envied her the matter of fact way she moved, organising people and things in the Guild, Church and Community, gathering fees, fares and dues from people as though greatly favouring them.

One thing particularly fascinated me for long was her name Annie S Telfer. For no known reason the "S" intrigued me.

One day I asked her "What does the 'S' stand for?"

"For one of my ancestors, William Skirving, one of the Scottish Martyrs of the 18th century. You'll have heard of them, Mr Lister?"

I had happened to be at the "Calton Hill" in Edinburgh a short time before and read on the 90ft obelisk there, the words on it:

> "To the memory of Thomas Muir, Thomas Fyshe Palmer, William Skirving, Maurice Margarot, Joseph Gerrard - Erected by the Friends of Parliamentary Reform in England and Scotland 1844"

On the other side was inscribed:

> *"I have devoted myself to the cause of the people.*
> *It is a good cause - it shall ultimately prevail; it shall finally triumph."*

Speech of Thomas Muir, in Court of Justiciary 30 August 1793.

Miss Telfer smiled "Yes, that William Skirving, was my ancestor" - just a trace of proud triumph in her voice.

Two hundred years ago was a time of change as this is. Freedom was known by its absence. Anger at those in power was rising to boiling point. In the age of George III and Lord Bute, his Foreign Secretary, the American colonists were rebelling, France ready to explode and good people's patience at breaking point.

In October 1793 a "Friends of the People" convention of reformers met and was constituted in Edinburgh. They were seven in number including a lawyer, a minister, teachers and church elders. They stated their aims of constitutional change, universal suffrage and some form of organisation to help the poor. The Whig administration declared them wreckers, traitors and criminals. A jury of fifteen persons prejudiced in favour of the British constitution's status quo, sentenced them to banishment in Botany Bay, New South Wales, Australia for fourteen years with no right of return.

Skirving at his trial said "It long since I laid aside the fear of man as my rule, I shall never walk by it. I know that what has been done these two days will be re-judged, this is my comfort and hope." The London Morning Post of 17 January 1794 reported "Mr Skirving in Scotland who was lately sentenced to fourteen years transportation leaves a wife and eight helpless children behind him." The Edinburgh Advocate, Peter MacKenzie said of Thomas Muir "A nobler man lives not this day within the city walls."

In banishment as in Scotland the martyrs' greatness showed. In his report of 16 October 1795 Governor Hunter wrote well of "the gentlemen whom Edinburgh magistrates provided for our colony. Mr Skirving appears to me a sensible well informed man, fond of farming and has purchased a piece of ground and makes good use of it which will by and by turn to his advantage." In one of his letters home to his wife Skirving evicted from his farm "Strathruddie" wrote, "I have given the name of "New Strathruddie" to this far away farm. I trust to make it soon of more value than the old. As Joseph Gerrard put it "Though justice steals with woollen feet she stitches at last with iron hands."

On 3rd March 1832 the Reform Bill was passed enfranchising many men in new towns, but still leaving power in the hands of the landed aristocracy - a significant first step. On 21st August 1844 the Scotsman reported "3,000 people assembled in the old Calton burial ground a few hundred yards from Holyrood Palace the ancestral home of Scottish kings. 400 members of the Complete Suffrage Association" in black had marched four abreast from Parliament Square by the Law Courts where the Patriots had received their unmerited sentences; down High Street and along the North Waterloo Bridges. They were welcomed by Mr Hume and Mr Skirving a manufacturer in Kirkcaldy son of one of the martyrs and again on 1st October 1845 "Last Friday the monument to commemorate the Scottish Martyrs of 1793-1795 was erected. The architect, Mr Hamilton, modelled it on Cleopatra's Needle in London. A stone was laid my Mr Joseph, MP about 20ft from David Hume's vault.

Recently in Australian Frank Clune's book "The Scottish Martyrs" I saw the photograph of William Skirving. I was amazed at the striking physical and facial resemblance to his most worthy descendant Annie S Telfer of Lundin Links, Fife. So the same Great Spirit lives on.

Chapter 12

THE DARK SIDE OF THE MOON

There are some places that have a quiet beauty about them; that make you feel this mustn't be spoiled. If it can be improved on; that is worth doing; but it shouldn't be damaged at all.

I felt this about the church in Upper Largo and the area round about it. But there was a piece of ground near it that amazed me. It was at the foot of the North Feus, an untidy patch of waste ground.

One night in early April 1970 I was standing on it chatting to some boys. "I wish we could do something to tidy up this place a bit" I heard myself say.

"Why not?" the boys said, in one voice to my surprise.

"We could make a garden of it" said Mel Berwick."

"That's a good idea" chimed in young Peter Rogers.

We met next night. It was a lovely warm spring evening - we had spades and barrows. We discussed what to do; and got stuck into it never doubting we were doing a useful bit of work; we were enjoying it just fine. Marion had given me a packet of biscuits and a flask of coffee.

We met the next two nights. We were making progress and enjoying that and each other's company. Something else had suddenly and worryingly caught the world's attention. The Space Age was well under way. Fascinated by it, but apprehensive how it might go, we discussed it often. At services we'd thought and prayed about it and linked it to the Christian Faith.

"The Eagle has landed" Neil Armstrong had shouted when Apollo XI had touched down on the Moon's Tranquillity Base on 20th July 1969.

"That is one small step for man, one great leap for mankind" were the no doubt well rehearsed words. Armstrong said when he himself set foot on the moon.

The race for the stars; landings on and possible settlement on other worlds seemed on course. But that spring day alarm and fear entered suddenly and chillingly into the thought and conversation of the world.

Apollo 13 had launched off into space. All was going well as she circled the moon with astronauts James Lovell, Fred Haise and Jack Swigert on board. Out of the blue a sentence from James Lovell to Mission Control, Houston, shocked the world, "Houston, we have a problem!"

It was our second night working on the piece of waste ground. Everybody's thoughts were on that patch of space that we'd never heard of before. As far as we were concerned it didn't exist. It did now; for us, for the world. The astronauts were in it, "The dark side of the moon." They were there. They were stuck in it and desperately wanted to get out of it. We, the worldlings wanted them out of it; hoped and prayed they would.

We worked away in our little piece of waste ground in Upper Largo; we were "on the dark side of the moon" with them.

"I wonder how they're getting on in Apollo 13?" I said to Mel.

"I dunno, I think I'm praying for them."

We all were, as we parted and agreed to meet next night.

As I opened the manse kitchen door, Marion said, with concern in her voice "There's been a bad accident on the Kirkaldy-Leven Road. Four Lundin Links boys have been injured, two quite badly." I knew them well, all good lads. Stephen Bayne, Derek Ovenstone, Philip Toothill and Allan Stuart. I phoned their homes and promised to visit in the morning which I did. Derek, quite badly injured, was in Kirkcaldy Royal Infirmary. I visited him later in the day. He was stretched out hanging face down in a hammock. "Your back looks all right!" I comforted him. He wasn't too bad. "I'm afraid you'll live D" I said with feeling.

There was no good news from the heavens. I always ended visits with a brief prayer whatever the circumstances. I prayed for the boys on Apollo 13 and bade Derek "Good bye." Derek never forgave me.

"Mr Lister visited me. He said a prayer. Not a word in it for me. He prayed just for the blooming astronauts." Derek made a splendid recovery. And so did the astronauts to the delight of themselves and the millions of us; their earth bound friends.

Apollo 13 was free from its darkness into the light of the sun again.

Gene Kranze, Head of Mission Control, Houston, and his cool headed, hard working team, in contact and cooperation with Apollo's crew completed their operation successfully.

As they had teased it out together one of the team had turned to Gene Kranze questioning the outcome. He answered calmly, smiling with confidence "Failure is not an option."

We completed our job. We had turned a piece of untidy wasteland into a pleasant rose garden. I happened to be back years later. I was pleased - the rose garden in bloom was beautiful. The Community Council had improved on it. To mark the Silver Jubilee of the Queen's Coronation, they had planted a tree. I remember looking at it, beautiful in its small way in the evening sun; with its royal look. The boys had done a good job.

I've often remembered the boys digging happily; the "Apollo 13" men in distress, Derek, prayerless himself, praying for others; and the bit of ground made some better. Even "on the dark side of the moon," "failure is not an option."

I found myself thinking of a good friend Donald Caskie "The Tartan Pimpernel". Donald came from Bowmore on the lovely island of Islay. Marion's forebears on her mother's side came from "The Lotts" Bowmore.

In 1940 Donald slipped out of Paris where he was minister of the Scots Kirk. Hitler's troops had broken through the Siegfried Line overrun France and taken Paris. Donald stayed with his congregation, but operated from the Seamen's Mission in Marseilles. With the help of a French Pastor Freunzy he organised "escape-routes" for service men and women, through Spain to Gibraltar. They saved hundreds of lives.

In the end the Gestapo caught up with Donald. He was arrested and imprisoned, under sentence of death in several concentration camps. He was interrogated and tortured. In the Villa Lynwood at Nice with others he was prepared for execution. From the cells he could hear the screams of friends being tortured as he had been.

He listened anxiously as his best friend Hakim was tortured. Hideous screams split the air; a brave man tortured beyond endurance. The beating had gone on for an hour and a half. Left in his cell Hakim's body was wracked with terrible pain. Donald was distressed by his demented sobbing. Then the weird deep seated weeping ceased. In the long silence Caskie feared his friend had died. But after the silence there came a sound of music weak, halting then stronger and sure the tune and the words of Bach's Passion Chorale.

"O sacred head sore wounded
With grief and shame weighed down
O kingly head surrounded
With thorns Thine only crown
How pale art thou with anguish
With sore abuse and scorn
How does that visage languish
Which once was bright as morn?"

Donald and his fellow prisoners were rescued at, for them, the eleventh hour. Failure, not an option; by faith and courage they 'had' won through, from the dark side of the moon.

> *The waste places will turn to a garden*
> *The sad places sound with song*
> *In company with a man of sorrow*
> *The darkness turns to light*
> *And day dawns with hope and promise.*

Caskie and his fellow prisoners were released as the allied armies, defeating the enemy and remembering them returned to release them. Donald lived out his days quietly as a minister of the Church in Scotland.

Chapter 13

MARION

"I'm late, Douglas," said Marion as she passed me at speed on the Ardbeg Road one Sunday morning. She was on her way to the Baptist Church where she was Organist. It was a mile's walk from her home on Rothesay Esplanade seafront. She had taken up her job as Organist in succession to her mother Anna Read who had done it efficiently and well for many years.

I noticed her legs that morning. They were not the long elegant lissom like legs that women like to display seductively from highish chairs; in any appropriate gathering, their skirts just above the knees. They were nice legs. It was the purposefulness of them that got my attention, and always held my attention afterwards.

I knew that she had done a full days work on Sunday before she had thought of her Organ playing duty at the local Baptist Church. The hotel, "Riversdale" which her father, Eddie Read, mother and herself, with a couple of maids help, ran, was full, with a mixture of holidaymakers, and Service personnel. It was Wartime, and Rothesay and the Island of Bute was a hub of activity with Army No. 9 Commandos, Officers and men of the Cyclops Submarine Supply ship; Naval Landing Craft crews and, of late, quite a smattering of Polish Army Officers.

Marion set the tables first thing; rang the Rising Bell along the hotel corridors, prepared breakfasts for 40 guests; served the breakfasts at the tables, and shared in tidying and washing up afterwards.

"Then, I'd better be going, Dad!" she'd say. Her brisk walk out the Ardbeg Shore by Rothesay Bay followed. It was then I heard her remark "I'm late, Douglas!"

I couldn't but think of the contrast. I had risen quietly on the Sabbath; read my passage for the day from "The Daily Light"; breakfasted, prayed a little, and walked slowly into the town and along to Church.

Zest for life, full participation in its personal and social activities with a wise, honest and courteous practical cheerfulness; that was Marion.

We'd been at school in Rothesay Academy together; she a Class ahead of me. I'd remembered her playing Schubert's "Marche Militaire" on the School Hall piano as the Classes marched into school. I'd been pleased when she invited me with her school Class to a Party at Riversdale. Her parents had gone out for the night, and left the Hotel to us. We had had quite a night. Games took us into every darkest and most remote nook and cranny in the building. We enjoyed ourselves.

The Hotel was never quite the same.

And now, by a quirk of fate, with my mother's choice of the Rothesay Baptist Church, our lives met up again. I joined the Choir; enjoyed being in such good company as the Organist's was. Marion used to rehearse after Choir Practice. I stayed with her and listened to her playing, perhaps pieces from "The Messiah," "He shall feed his flock, like a shepherd," "Sheep may safely graze" and the like. We liked being together. We had walks or cycle runs across lovely island ways. In the house afterwards she'd play her repertoire of pieces. Chopin's Nocturnes were my favourites. Then at a Concert in the Living Room one night her singing of "I'm owre young, I'm owre young, I'm owre young to marry yet, I'm owre young 'twad be a shame. To tak' me frae my mammy yet!" wakened me from sleeping. We courted. We enjoyed it, except for the midges, their unacceptable places and ways. I wasn't much good; a platonic sort of talker and walker, not much of a lover.

One weekend I came down from Glasgow. "Marion is engaged to a Lieutenant Commander in the Navy, a Lt. Commander Mansell Davies "my mother remarked. I'd felt our relationship hadn't been going as it should, and the fault was mine, I was sad with a stoical sadness.

In time Marion broke her engagement. Coming into the shop for messages, she was her usual brilliant self. We took up again. On the night of V.J. Day August 14th–after a twenty six mile hike along the Cowal Shore by Loch Striven, I proposed to Marion. We married in Ardbeg Baptist Church on 14th November, 1945 the Rev. D. Gunn Sutherland, the Officiating Minister.

Marion was an only child. Her father from Evercreeh in Somerset was one of a family of nine; the only one of them to marry. He had come North to train as an engineer, staying with his Uncle Charles Smith in Ascog Bute. Her mother was an only child, from a family in Bowmore in the Island of Islay Her forebears had long been in Islay as her husband to be's family had been in Somerset. Eddie had met Anna walking along the promenade by Rothesay Bay; and the pleasant Anglo-Scottish alliance born there led to a happy marriage and useful life. Marion was the finest child of really fine parents.

No Minister of the Church of Scotland was more fortunate in his wife, than I was in Marion.

The Family, Christmas 1975

Does the Church of Scotland appreciate the worth it has had and has in its Ministers wives?

Marion had left school at fifteen and proceeded to obtain her L.R.A.M. and A.R.C.M. diplomas under the tuition of Miss Aggie Millar of Glasgow. In addition she had acted and worked as partner with her father and mother in their hotel business. She was then, in the thirty one years of our marriage, to give herself with complete dedication and skill to serve the Church; a Minister's wife, running the Manse, entertaining Members and Visitors acceptably, raising the family, acting as Organist and Choirmistress as required; singing in the Choir, leading Organisations; and being in effect a Minister to the Congregation; as good as and in some ways more effective than the Minister himself. And for no kind of remuneration; except the reward and the pain of sharing the whole Ministry of the Church itself.

This means there is considerably more than the ordinary weight of the husband-wife responsibility, with quite a deal more added.

For two hundred years after the Reformation, the Minister's wife was normally called, and regarded as "The Priest's Woman" There seems to me

69

no good reason whatever why today's Priests, if they so wish, should have such a "Woman"; such a sweetheart, lover, wife.

This has been the priceless asset of most Ministers and their Congregations.

Marion was fortunate that, on such occasions as I was moving and without house, she and later the family could retreat to the comfort of her parents house in Rothesay.

Abroad in Post War Germany, she gave leadership, friendship and wise encouragement to Forces personnel and Germans alike. In Egypt she was a friend to many Egyptians and a wise inspiration to all "Suez Contractor" and civilian personnel.

In Carnoustie, in Inverurie and in Largo her presence was always an encouragement and a memorable benediction.

On July 5th 1975 I had intended going the next day to Carnoustie for the Open Golf Championship, and to be with some old friends. But something made me hesitate and stay at home. Next evening, late at night, Marion crawled downstairs in great pain. This, I sensed, was the beginning of serious trouble. Throughout the ensuing cancer, her courage and gentle cheerfulness were a continuous inspiration. I recently came on my Diary for those days. Day after day is marked by the faith and hope of a good person. The entry for April 16th, Good Friday tells that her favourite young Doctor, Dr. Kumyeh, a Palestinian from Nablus, has told her that no more can be done to cure her. "If you can't do anything you can't do anything. I'll try to be cheerful." Two days later I note she said "Let there be no gloom on my account. I'm curious to know what the future will be like. I'll come as close to you as I can. We've had such a happy time, and been so fortunate and lucky." And to 11 year old Alice, she said "I'm sorry I'm leaving you like this; and won't see the beautiful girl you'll become but try not to be too sad." She maintained a spirit of irrepressible cheerfulness and optimism to the end on 10th May 1976.

As she slipped into unconsciousness she whispered with feeling, "It has been such a lovely time." Thousands mourned her dying at 56, as the loss of a true and good friend. She was, without shadow of doubt, a Minister's ideal wife.

Basically she was too good for her husband Minister. His serious fault was that he was not emotionally mature enough for her. And try as he might and did, he failed sexually and spiritually, to be to her the husband she deserved and needed to have. He was, he discovered, made that way, and did not and could not change sufficiently. He regretted the lack in himself, which his wife knew, but which she denied.

In a sense his faults were not unique to him. He was a "driven" man, married to the Church; eager to do his job well, anxious to succeed. At times, he felt he was by nature a celibate priest. The loss was in the affection, love and enjoyment his wife and family should have known, of which they were in fact deprived.

David Anderson was a nice enough man, a Carnoustie Elder and Clothier. He had one habit that greatly annoyed me. He enjoyed speaking, and, as he spoke, he smoked. He left his cigarette in his mouth till the ash fell off on to his shirt. "How's your one day a week job?" he asked me, one day as he smoked.

I was really angry. I prided myself on the work I did, and got done. I kept an exact diary of my on-duty hours for the next three months; and published the findings in the Parish Magazine, as a rebuttal of David's "one day a week" charge. I was on duty a hundred hours a week, every week.

With hindsight I recognised and realise several things. I was neglecting my wife and my family quite seriously.

David had caught me on the hop. He was no doubt joking; teasing rather than rebuking. I was taking myself too seriously and too vainly.

I missed the point. The right thing was to love the Lord, the Church, my family and myself sensibly, by working a little less hard and long, to relax, easeup, love and laugh more and not less.

Life is about jobs and the right doing of them. But without love and a laugh as we go, they may be seriously in vain.

I should have learned to love my wife more. She had it right.

I'm sorry, dear.

Chapter 14

THE CHURCH OF SCOTLAND

The gude auld Kirk o' Scotland,
The wild winds round her blaw,
And when her foemen hear her sough,
They prophecy her fa;
But what although her fate has been
Amang the floods to sit –
The gude auld Kirk o' Scotland,
She's nae in ruins yet!-

George Murray, 1819-1868

We do ourselves no good, nor anybody else; if we are fulsome in self-praise.

Fortunately for herself and Scotland; Scotland's Church, in my experience of her, has always been highly critical of herself and her work on the ground. That is how I've found her, in over fifty years of trying to serve her. That is how she is, how I like her and how I hope she will stay.

"Scotland's Church" is not, in her case, I submit a misnomer; for while she is, by law established, her "national" Church; she is "independent" and interdenominational and internationally minded. Scotland's people are her main if not her sole concern.

Whether we have served the common people who heard Jesus gladly as truly and well as our forebears is the only critique that is valid.

Commending Jesus Christ to people in humble and true service, has always been my preference to going of set purpose to "convert" them to our way of thinking. And this is being well done in a variety of fine ways today. An example of that Sandra and I enjoyed the other day in the fine village of Tarves nearby.

A very fine assistant to Inverurie doctor James Gill, Gordon Laing served his practice in Tarves well; until retiring. I noticed he was going out to Ekwendeni to practice on a short-term basis in Malawi. Tarves village put on a weekend's events to raise money to support Gordon and Kathleen Laing in Malawi. Sandra and I went to join in the celebrations. Part of the holy hilarity was the new Minister Leslie Barrett and his son Andrew duetting skilfully and beautifully on their sanctified bagpipes.

It was as "holy" a "fair" as I can remember. That slightly more relaxed way of serving our fellow men and women in our new age I find refreshing and right; "Communion" together, celebrating as one family the "grace of God" for our saving; and sharing the joy and benefit of it with one another. "Laughter in the Aisles."

Some of the amusing Moments in Public Worship I was always to find the most reverent. Laughter and a smile that accompanied the seeming irreverence of human frailty in the House of God.

One summer, taking Services in the beautiful village of Plockton in Wester Ross, office bearers used to regale me with stories of one of their Ministers, a Mr Nicolson. They had obviously loved him. He had a son, called Torquil and he had cattle grazing in a field beside the Manse Garden. The Church, like the one at Towie in Donside, had the pulpit high up on the long wall. From it there was a good view of the Manse Garden through a window. One Sunday the Public Worship of God was proceeding with due solemnity. Mr Nicolson's Prayer of Adoration had just achieved "lift off" "As the Lord said to Moses" intoned Mr Nicolson, "Torquil, will ye get they cattle out of the Manse Garden." Torquil was a big and obedient boy. The cattle, like the first transgressors Adam and Eve, duly sworn at and excommunicated from the Plockton Manse garden, peace reigned for a time.

On another occasion Mr Nicolson announced, "Let us worship God in Psalm One Hundred and Twenty Four" - "Torquil will ye close that door."

I met Torquil years later, at a wedding in Largo. He was a giant of a man, in full tartan regalia. He was then Executive of Highland Region. "Were these stories true, about your father?" I asked him. "Yes, and there were a lot more" he replied.

Irreverent too were three worshippers in Largo. In the back pew of the North Transept of Largo's rather beautiful old Church, three highly intelligent and mischievously obstreperous ladies enjoyed a most interesting gossip before the sharing of any Godspell. Jean Muriset, Maisie Clark and Chrissie Anderson, all from Lundin Links were the "unholy trinity" in question.

It was I knew difficult for them to be respectfully serious ever; for their daily conversations with their Minister tended to be light-heartedly irreverent on most occasions of meeting. This was mutually acceptable on

73

weekdays; and Sunday Worship tended to be for them a continuation of weekdays encounter with their rather human Minister rather than a meeting with the Most High and holy One. Jean Muriset I have to admit was the worst offender. With her husband Freddie she had built up a most successful business as Proprietrix of the Lundin Links Hotel, in "The Madeira of Scotland." She had a fantastic sense of humour, and was no respecter of persons, least of all Ministers. Marion, my wife, and Jean got on like a house on fire, and I, and Jean's charming but slightly old worldie husband Freddie, were regularly and most impiously burned at their completely disrespectful feminine stakes.

The "terrible trinity" gathered religiously, on each Sabbath morning in their favourite back pew.

After most unholy but enjoyable gossip, they put on their falsely reverent faces. The commencement of sermon was the signal for friendly jollification. Sweets passed from one lady to another with sounds of appreciation. Knowing that I had sweated long hours of blood on the Word of God they seemed to regard as little more than a rather poor amateurish, badly performed Circus Act, I, did my best but clearly with some difficulty. One day I found myself, partly jealous partly peeved. I intervened in my divine flow with some-such words as, "I have over the years studied the various means by which members enjoy the pleasure of eating a sweet during time of sermon. Some piously bend their heads, and insert the desired piece of confectionery. Others cover their mouth for a cough and enjoy the fruit of their deception. Others seek defence and supposed invisibility sitting behind a pillar. I sympathise with those devious means of mingling pleasure with pain. But one thing I find mean and discourteously distracting is the unwrapping of sweets in crinkly paper and the ungodly passing of the noisily unwrapped sweet to one's most undevout pew-fillers!"

The sweet-eating ladies, the offenders in question, got the message. Jean Muriset, Maisie Clerk and Chrissie Anderson solemnly nodded in worshipful agreement. The next Sunday, before commencement of worship, Mrs. Muriset beckoned me over to their back pew, remarking, "Will that do then, Douglas?" She pointed to a row of twenty to thirty delicious sweets along the pew. They had all been unwrapped.

I never tried to win. It was quite impossible. I enjoyed mischief and humour too much to try. Jesus seemed to be rather like that too. We're only human. We don't have long to stay. Let's enjoy ourselves together in the time we have together. That I think was the real Jesus.I reckoned and reckon. He, I think, likes the Church to be the same. That was to be how I found it."

SOME OF MY FAVOURITE MINISTERS

The fact that several of them have been "Moderators" quite clearly reflects how it has been and is important. Scotland's antipathy to Bishops and a too hierarchically structured Church is a result of England's long warfare and tyrannical approach over the centuries and the Stuart kings' use of "Episcopacy" as their weapon with which to make a proud and obstinate people knuckle under. That Scotland never did and never would do.

"No bishops; no king" was Charles I's feeblest piece of armoury. English arrogance and bullying was, as it usually is, successfully counter-productive. Like Scotland herself, Scotland's church encouraged friendship, camaraderie and comradeship. "No bishops" was true but we all regarded ourselves, a little stupidly perhaps, as "bishops." The word only means "supervisor" or "Shepherd." But we recognised and respected our betters and superiors. They offered their help as brothers in Christ. I for one was to appreciate and enjoy that.

Among the many whose friendship and advice I was to come to treasure were Ministerial "greats"; many of them "Moderators" equal, who treated every one else as "equals"; so that friendship, trust and the sense of being real "colleagues" developed happily and naturally.

This is one of the happier results of the Reformation; the emphasis on it being treated by God, on the example and emphasis of Jesus of Nazareth, as on the level; and trying to keep it that way. I sometimes wonder if my idea of becoming a Minister began one day in Riversdale Hotel, Rothesay. I had gone in to have a word with Marion whose parents owned the hotel. She herself was a very important factor in its success. The local "Ministers Fraternal" used to meet there. On the coat-stand in the Hall was an array of Ministerial hats. One belonging to a yachtsman Minister Mr Dunlop Brown caught my attention. It was the broad rimmed, shallow variety of hat. I tried it on and liked it. "Oh, that suits you, Douglas!" laughed Marion. I think she first entertained the idea that she might be a Minister's wife, from that moment!

I found the Rothesay Ministers a really great bunch of men. The happy conversation and the gales of hearty laughter that carried into the Hall of the hotel raised my esteem of the Ministry in my boyish imagination.

But at the same time it didn't take me long, after my Ordination to realise that many of our Ministers and Moderators were of as high a calibre as many of Britain's best Prime Ministers, Judges, Civil Servants and Business Executives. Some were clearly better. They had chosen the Ministry as the way of serving Scotland in the name of Christ independently of private and personal gain and fame.

I genuinely found it an interesting and enriching pleasure to share life with them as equals in the "Internationale" of Christ. That was the feel of the Church of Scotland that I got from the start. It was never to leave me. I came on the scene at the end of the great John White's Ministry. If anyone, could have been a great leader, at the highest rank of any nation, John White was that man. He commanded; he led - knowing well that he did. Perhaps not always altogether agreeing, the Church was willing to be wisely led. One of White's greatest concerns and successes was to reunite the "old" Church of Scotland and "the Free Church" of the Disruption of 1843. He succeeded and the Church scored a useful success in unity with him.

The brightest star, in Scotland, in the 20th century was, I have to say, Lord Macleod of Fiunary, George Macleod. No one quite made the impact for good often in the face of fierce opposition I think as George did. I've never known anyone who so treated you on the level as George did.

And no one, did, or could do what we needed done, restore the vision and the heart of the early Celtic Church - not just "soul" salvation, but "whole" salvation, as he did "The Son of Man" for the sons and daughters of man; body soul and spirit and mind - "The Full Monty." Jesus the Carpenter of Nazareth for the elite of Edinburgh and the shipyard workers and unemployed of Govan. Jesus the carpenter, God of the working man was a vital emphasis. That is how it was. That is how it is. George put that centre stage again for the Church and people of Scotland.

That's only part of the debt we owe him. "Thank you George."

The two Ministers I loved most across the years were Kenneth MacKenzie of Strathpeffer and James Matheson of Portree.

I had never met; and have never met; anyone who was at once so sincerely charming, good looking, highly intelligent, mentally active, interesting, courteous, amusing and utterly humble at one and the same time. as Kenneth MacKenzie.

Kenneth MacKenzie

Kenneth was born on 29th June 1920; seven days before me. From a very fine family, Kenneth grew up happily and progressed brilliantly with his education from Dingwall Academy, Aberdeen University and New College Edinburgh, through Inter Varsity Fellowship to the Mission field on which his heart had long been set. Ken met and married his student sweetheart Margaret Torrance. Margaret still lives in Edinburgh.

Kenneth was to make his mark on Africa and leave it long to be remembered because he so loved people and understood the Africans and so resented British political policies to maintain unjust rule over the native population.

The Church of Scotland by then was wholly on the side of freedom and justice for the world's oppressed and enslaved. I remember Stuart McWilliam, then of Wellington Church, Glasgow and I myself in Inverurie and with many other Ministers being mocked and criticised for our support for the liberation of African natives, American Negroes and earth's coloureds. It was considered a form of disloyalty bordering as "traitorous" in some quarters. It never was that.

Kenneth's particular campaign was against the British Government's plan to join Nyasaland, Northern and Southern Rhodesia in a "Central African Federation" - a British white block in the heart of Africa. Sir Roy Welensky a former boxer was appointed to see it through. He had not reckoned on Kenneth with his encyclopaedic knowledge of the situation and his passion for human justice, nor with the Church of Scotland. Kenneth informed the Church and the country of the facts. The General Assembly roundly and consistently exposed the stupidity and wrong of the plan. The Government, under such scrutiny and pressure reluctantly recanted. Ian Smith, in all white Southern Rhodesia did a ridiculous Declaration of Independence act. Harold Wilson in the end called his bluff.

Kenneth, I shall never forget nor the shock of his all too early death. Kenneth served with his usual excellence as Minister of Restalrig Parish Church from 1968. He died there in February 1971; all too prematurely for all who knew him, and for Scotland. I shall never forget either, after the service in the church was over, the picture of a very handsome African leaning over one of the ancient stones in the Restalrig graveyard crying his eyes out. The loss of Kenneth Mackenzie, faithful and outstanding Minister of the Church and the best friend Africa ever had was greater than he could bear.

James Matheson

James Matheson I never got to know well. I always hoped I would. We only had one or two conversations; but as with John Althorp that was enough. He had a quality of quiet and most moving wisdom and goodness about him. The beauty of the gentle lilt of is voice and manner won over all who knew him, it was just a joy to be with him. After ten years in Knox Church Dunedin, he returned to Scotland and persuaded Scotland's Church to be generous in a great cause. He was Secretary of the Stewardship and Budget Committee of the Church from 1961 till 1973. He was Moderator in 1975-1976.

Roy Sanderson

Crieff Hydro, at which under the Meikle Trust Ministers and their wives could enjoy a holiday at reduced terms and in good company was long popular with Marion and our family. There we met one of the pleasantest of Ministers and his wife Muriel, Roy Sanderson. Roy was Moderator in 1967.

In late 1960's the Editor of "Life and Work" whom I liked a lot. Leonard Bell fell out of favour with members of his committee. They wished him removed from his job. I was on the Publications Committee, which dealt with these issues at the time. I considered Leonard had been running the magazine as a sort of Church Scots Magazine which suited him. Some did not consider his approach was sufficiently serious, evangelical and spiritual. His lighter touch suited me fine. I also thought that as the Editor's appointment was by the General Assembly, it was its responsibility and not the committee's to hire and fire.

I was in a minority of two. Angus Nicholson, a former Chaplain was the other. Leonard appealed to the Assembly and won his case. He had a bad heart; and heart broken he died soon after. I never really forgave my more "spiritual" churchmen.

In the middle of the dispute Roy Sanderson who loved being on the side of sense and justice phoned me. We agreed to meet in Edinburgh. We were both dressed smartly, dog collars and all. We were walking down to Princes Street when two very professional, black suit and hatted gentlemen; one big, bluff and stout; the other a minute black copy - little and large approach. The big one (yin) greeted us as long lost bosom friends. "Come up to my office for a drink." I looked at Roy. He sort of nodded. In the untidiest of lawyers offices which really was saying a lot; from under his desk the big one drew out a bottle of whisky and a bottle of sherry. "Our wives are teetotal so we have to take our pleasures here."

The big one came from Lewis. "I'm not religious you know." He covered the religious front more than we knew talking by now loudly as he went on and on.

We at last excused ourselves. He rose to spray Roy's mouth with some alcohol odour eliminator. The wee one tried to do the same for me. I brushed him off. "I like the taste of whisky!" I remarked.

Glad to be free we went down the stair. "Where on earth did you meet these two?" I joked with Roy. "I never set eyes on them. I thought you knew them" remarked Roy smiling in the characteristically shy and amusing way he always did.

We had many happy hours with Roy and Muriel. But that I think was the most memorable and amusing.

Peter Brodie

Peter Brodie was Moderator in 1978. He had been through the war parachuting into the horror of Arnhem. I liked Peter and shared many a happy hour with him. With his bright intellect, warm humanity; love of life and immense good humour he was encouragement personified. His main Ministry was in St Mungo's Church Alloa but in the administration of the Church he was the most reliable of colleagues.

Among other memorable incidents; in his Moderatorial year, one has remained high in its pleasure giving content. He visited McIntosh's the Kirkcaldy furniture firm. The owner, our near neighbour and friend in Upper Largo, a good Baptist Bill McIntosh greeted him and introduced him to Tom Robertson, the firm's chief designer. Tom and his wife, Elizabeth, were a wonderful pair. Tom a good Presbyterian youth met quiet, lovely Catholic girl at a dance. They met often after and married. Tom became a good Catholic with a fine family of nine.

Great raconteur and actor, Peter Brodie, solemnly recounted to Bill and Tom the story of the "Great Church Robbery." Some months before while a court was in session in the General Assembly Hall the Edinburgh police intervened. "May we have your permission, Sir, to remove the Moderator's three chairs and the chairs of the Ex-Moderators - the centre piece of the Assembly?" queried the Chief Constable of the Sheriff. "Certainly Sir." The furniture firm moved the chairs into their quality van. The thief of the old chairs was found and convicted, but the property, thought to have gone to Holland was not recovered.

Mr McIntosh was the kindest of men. He turned to his chief designer, "Tom could we help out?" "I think so, Sir," replied Tom, Peter Brodie protested, expostulated in fact! Covered with confusion and delight.

On a visit to the site of the crime Tom Robertson saw a very valuable French Chippendale chair. "Why did they not take that one?" he asked. "The Sheriff was sitting on it!" replied the Chief Clerk.

Tom designed and made fifteen new chairs for the Church of Scotland's Assembly Hall. The team of craftsmen involved comprised Brian Robertson, carver, Mr Alison and Mr John Graham, cabinet makers, Mr Finlay Thain, upholsterer and Mr Balfour McGrory, polisher and managing director Robert Adams. Bill and his firm McIntosh of Kirkcaldy gifted them to the Church of Scotland. Until the new buildings are ready they will be at the heart of the new Scottish Parliament.

They are quality chairs. The design, Tom, inspired by Rennie McIntosh, created a modern burning bush; topped by a dove. The back is in blue. The legs are sculptured with thistles; signs of bread and wine and the Saltire or St Andrew's cross. For comfort they are made in the ergonomic style.

The new chairs in the Assembly Hall are themselves prophetic of the future that should have been our past. Suggested by Peter the Church of Scotland's Moderator; made by the skill of Tom Robertson, good young Protestant, inspired by faith and love into a good Roman Catholic by Elizabeth his wife; and donated freely to the Church of Scotland by an able and generous minded Baptist, Bill McIntosh.

Peter Brodie's Moderatorship was also marked by a visit to the General Assembly of Pope John. Looking them together, I felt they could easily have exchanged jobs. Peter died after a long and painful illness. That, he did not deserve.

Appropriate I think it is that the Scottish Church's motto is the Burning Bush of Moses, and the words of that desert meeting "Nec Consumebatur." "It was not consumed." A sign and symbol for Scotland's future.

As I look back, names of many gifted, good, true and fine men and women - Johnstone-Jeffrey, Craig, Macleod, Henderson, Macintyre, Fraser, Whyte, Davidson, McVicar, Doig, MacLuskey, McIndoe, McDonald Torrance and Main come to mind. Remembering pleasant people makes the present brighter and the future hopeful. We are a people greatly in debt.

The view of John's Holy City was of "a great assembly; whom no one could number." That I suppose is about it. One thing I do know is that Scotland has been fortunate indeed in the men and women of the last century who have served her in her Church.

Chapter 15

"COMBINED OPERATIONS"
CHRISTIANS PLEASE

The state of inter-Church relations when I was a boy was more or less what it is in Ulster today. And although I keep hoping for a breakthrough to sanity, which there should be; the murderous legacy of ignorance, bigotry and hate take long years to clear.

In Rothesay in the 20's there was the mutual distrust of prejudice between Protestant and Catholics. There were two sides, and for us, Catholics were on the enemy side. I was told of an Uncle who was under threat from Catholics in the town. A crowd of Catholics had it in for him. They arranged to meet in the Public Park up High Street. There they would lay wait, attack, do him up. He crossed the Lade Bridge at the end of the Park on his way home at night. A black eye, very sore head and a dip in the lade would be the least he would get. He escaped his no doubt deserved punishment. Significantly enough a couple of Catholic girls warned him of the plot, and no doubt saved his Protestant bacon.

A hundred yards down from Lister's Nurseries on Barone Road was a convent; in and out of which I used to see slightly menacing hooded ladies slowly or quickly move; called nuns. A very high and thick wall hid from view their secret, and of course suspect, missionary activities. I walked past the convent warily and circumspectly. I think I longed for a spy hole to plumb the depths of its Catholic designs.

One night I knew it all. I had a nightmare. I've never forgotten it. I wakened up screaming, my pyjamas soaked in good Protestant sweat. I was seven years old.

As I walked down Barone Road one early evening to the "Lifeboys" the pavement rocked and the stout Catholic wall caved in. Priests and nuns were dancing round a blazing, crackling fire. People I knew were lying on the ground trussed up. The man I seem to have adopted as my father figure, Sunday School Superintendent and Provost Angus Thomson, was being held up shoulder high ready to be the next Protestant barbecued person. Beyond the firelight of the flames, I heard from the darkness, the sinister sound of metal click on metal. I went towards it. Could it be? It was a guillotine, horror of horrors. My tiny neck began to tingle. I could not, I would not, believe it. Those scum-priests and nuns of quiet, saintly appearance - unholy murderers were going to guillotine the only person I could love, my beautiful, kind and absolutely lovely Aunt Alice.

I yelled out with mixed terror and anger. "What is it dear?" I heard a voice enquire. A limp frenzied little boy woke up. There are still moments when I relive it all; to its minutest detail.

Christianity, Rothesay style then, Ulster style still.

What started me then considering our position as Protestants were two things. First the claptrap of the songs we sang. A bunch of us saw Canon Butler walk along the road. I always liked his upright walk. We climbed through the Nursery Hedge on to the Meadow Road and sang "King Billy slew the Papist crew, at the battle of Boyne Water." Canon Butler turned and waved his stick at us. The Canon walked on. We sang louder. This time he turned and walked towards us. We retreated to the gooseberry bushes and the shelter of the raspberry canes.

Later I met Canon Butler and his housekeeper in the shop and delivered messages to the house out Craigmore. We exchanged greetings at the back door. He was a nice man.

Then at school, there were Catholics in the class. Margo Wogt and Jimmy Boyle. Margo was a lively girl. She flirted with me quite openly. If I hadn't been daft, I'd have enjoyed her company quite a lot.

Jimmy and I got on fine. His father was a bookie in the town; one leg off at the knee. He was a cheerful man with a hat and specs; a florid complexion and his book busily writing his bets as he sort of leaned on his crutch.

These were people as sensible and decent as anybody else. These things first made me feel the Protestant-Catholic divide was a bit daft but I was busy with my own affairs and quite happy in my "Evangelical" stream.

It stayed the same in Gibraltar. Happy with the outcome of the war; set in its British Establishment ways Romans, Episcopalians and others; doing their own separate thing enjoying individual recognition. Quite the nicest of men was the old handsome grey-haired altogether charming Methodist, Father Brown the troops called him.

Germany changed all that for me. Our Christian bombs had fallen. There was ruin, loss and pain everywhere. I felt quite clearly that in the face of such appaling human distress and need,the only right thing to do was for people who called themselves "Christian" to work together in the common cause of the One God and the poor people He'd given His Son to save.

Scotland since 1910 had taken the initiative in regarding us as "Brithers a" in sharing our Gospel, in the first meeting of the newly formed "Ecumenical" Movement ("ecumenical" being Greek for "Inhabited world") in Edinburgh. Sanity had at last crept up on the Christian Church and Germany and its peoples in their broken and distressed state, sent that signal to a young Army Chaplain up to his eyes in the mess of it all.

I had luck with the Episcopal chaplain in the Luneburg Garrison; Welshman Leslie Lloyd Jones. We divided up a job that needed five not two of us. Five thousand service personnel, nineteen Commanding Officer hours (30 to 300 service personnel to address and talk things over with at a time) each week, welfare work and the rest.

We shared Sunday Services. One Sunday Leslie would conduct the Anglican form of Service and I would take the lessons and Sermon. Next Sunday I would conduct in the Church of Scotland mode and Leslie would read lessons and preach.

These Services were fantastically popular. Rex de Winton the 4th Armoured Division Brigadier and Colonel Foote V.C. of 2nd Tanks; the Greys Colonel Ralph Younger and a good cross section of men and women and many children across the Garrison of several completely different denominations meeting, praying, worshipping as one - enjoyed what for them was quite new and magic experience. We shared the Sacraments too. That was 1947-48.

And working together was perhaps what mattered and helped most! I was never to forget the quizzical, mischievous glint in ex Luftwaffe Pilot Jo Makovec's eyes on our first meeting in 1947. He had come to plead for help for the refugees freezing to death in their ragged tent camp down by the river Elbe; 80,000 of them. "I have 5,000 souls in this garrison I've to try and help. What on earth more can I do?"

I can still see and hear Jo Macovec. He fixed me with a quiet, kindly but penetrating look and said "Perhaps you could get them to help!"

What I hadn't counted on was the flood of anonymous aid from Scotland that made essential help rewarding and immensely valuable.

Our congregations united in worship became united in Christian Aid and wouldn't have returned to their old ways if they'd been paid to do so. That experience of helping refugees in their loss and need made crystal clear to me that "combined operations" was the only sensible and right way for the future.

In 1949 St Stephen's Church in Scotland's East Coast town of Carnoustie the Roman Catholic Priest remained invisible and in isolation. But Canon Walter de Voil of the Episcopal Church was the light of our life. Small, round, tubby, with a smile on his face and almost always laughing with an infectious mirth and happy to co-operate not only in Christian Aid but everything; a real and good colleague. What a difference practical goodwill makes in life.

Again, Egypt, 1956, as Chaplain with the Suez Contractors was full of interest; none more pleasant than complete communion with the Anglican Church. I visited Bishop Frank Johnston in Cairo before my Anglican colleague came out. "I'd love to do things on a "combined operations" Ecumenical Principle," I said. "I entirely agree," said Frank. Michael Powell my Anglican colleague was a very honourable and excellent person not familiar with the Church of Scotland. But we shared everything more or less how Lloyd Jones and I had done in Luneburg; but more. We practised full "Inter-Communion." Bishop Johnston celebrated the Eucharist and we received it from his hands. I celebrated the Sacrament and he, Michael and the Anglican congregation received it from my hands. We communed, worshipped; learned each other's ways and knew ourselves mutually enriched. There was faith, no doubts about that, and it was great and right.

In recent years the Church has been slimmed down a bit. People, at the moment do not go because it's the "respectable" thing to do. They are more likely not to go than to go. The solemn stiffness of "officialdom" has lessened. People of different ages go because they want and need to go. They want to worship together. They enjoy the support of others - more obviously humble, natural and sincere; somehow, self-effacingly encouraging one another in a faith; a way of life that challenges comforts and encourages.

I think if that can be increased, sustained and maintained it will be for the good of all.

What I have only realised of late is not only that we are in the same boat on the same voyage with the same captain and going to the same harbourage; all the different branches of the Christian Church worship in the same form, almost exactly the same way.

I love the Salvation Army; I have friends in the Brethren, Abbey Fellowships, Baptist, Congregational, Lutheran, Orthodox, Coptic and Orthodox Churches.

The language may be different, the singing and the style of worship; but it's the same God and Lord Jesus Christ that we worship and promise to serve. We are under the same Master on the same crusade and with the same hope. That is also true of the Roman Catholic Church; a Church I have discovered is as rich in humility devotion and love as any other in the world. To move from the warmth of Egypt and Prison there, on our release at Christmas 1956 when the last of the British and French troops had left Egyptian soil, to Aberdeenshire in the north of Scotland was to experience something different. It was; but for me it was better; not only because of the warmth of Aberdeenshire people, but because of the Roman Catholic Priest, Father Alex Smith.

Alex was a clever, kindly cultured man with a rich vein of good humour. We welcomed him to our manse. We enjoyed having him. He enjoyed being with us and being musical he shared the pleasure of that at our grand piano with a kindred musical spirit, my wife Marion. He was a connoisseur of good food and Marion gave him that.

We were quite simply colleagues in the faith; battling on the same side.

He didn't like much that had been done by Roman Catholics in the name of Jesus Christ. I didn't like much that had been done by Protestants.

By the 1960's I knew that inter-Communion was the right thing for us. I had experienced the spiritual and social benefit of it in Fayid, Ismailia and Tel el Kebir in Egypt.

We are all in this together; uniting humbly seriously and hopeful with Jesus Presence working in his Spirit to make the devil go back to Hell where he belongs and let the caring, saving, healing way of Jesus of Nazareth to work in His world.

We can but work and pray to bring healing and sanity into a world that needs in those things.

So much progress in understanding and cooperation has been made.It makes sense to go forward and not move backward.

Angelo Guiseppe Roncalli was born on 25 November 1931; one of thirteen children born to Giovanni Roncalli; a tenant farmer in the village of Sotto il Monte in Lombardi. From 1958 - 1963 he was Pope of the Roman Catholic Church in Rome. He was just a lovely man. He spread his arms wide and said with all his heart "Welcome to Jesus." He didn't mean to the Roman way of things. He meant to Jesus who loves the world regardless of who you are, what you are, of whatever colour, class or creed.

The blessing of Pope John XXIII's attitude and Alex Smith's friendship was very real to all of us in the early sixties. Among Alex's gifts to us when we were leaving Inverurie in 1967 was a copy of "The Jerusalem Bible." In it was a Benediction of Rhabamus Mamus of the 12th Century.

"Do but remember me, as I do thee
And God who brought us into this world
Bring us together in His house of Heaven."

Alex died in his sleep of a heart attack not long after, aged 46. I still mourn his loss. Often in worship I have used his Benediction, each time sharing it with him.

In Largo, I was sorry to have no Priest with whom to share our Ministry, but happy with good colleagues. In 1995 there, we celebrated the founding of the settlement of the Celtic Aethernasus in the area 1,100 years before. We had a "Largo Festival" plays, concerts, including a memorable concert by Jean Redpath. But the highlight for us was the Sunday service in which

Ecumenical Service, Largo

Largo Colleagues Jim Mackenzie, Jo Campbell of the Baptist Church, Alex Watson, moderator of Presbytery, friend Kenneth MacVicar, Kenmore as preacher, Episcopal Archbishop Michael Hare Duke and Cardinal Gordon Gray joined to give thanks and dedicate ourselves as one; a full church, a great choir and a very happy time.

Gordon Gray was known and respected nation-wide as leader of the Roman Catholic Church in Scotland. He had agreed to take the first prayer only. Before the service I said to him "Please feel free to give us a brief word from your heart." He did. It was brief. It was absolutely lovely; the word of a humble, warm-hearted, faithful old servant of the Lord and his people. I have never forgotten Gordon Gray or his word. But he and his good influence will be his pleasant memorial for long in the land.

I only wish Ian Paisley and his kind could have been humble enough to learn his lesson. It is for me the clear lesson we have all sadly taken too long to learn. The breakthrough, I think is here.

Just as a great liner and huge tanker finds it difficult to go astern and change direction, it is most difficult for the Roman Catholic Church to adjust to the new unity that the Church and the world needs. It is extremely hard for any nation, people or organisation with a long and mostly noble and well loved tradition; and especially one that has believed it is the best and only true Church; to humbly and wisely co-operate with those who have opposed, condemned and waged war against them. It is doubly so, when they have made significant moves along the road of reconciliation and the fullest possible co-operation, to be other than angry with loud mouthed would be spiritual leaders who ignorantly continue to fight yesterday's three hundred year wars and look with unconcern on the appaling harvest of suffering and death of their ungodly preaching. They are joined in total agreement by sensible people of all faiths and of none.

That said, the Roman Catholic Church should now practice full inter-Communion with all peoples who sincerely love Jesus Christ. The Church of Scotland believes in the "real presence of Jesus Christ" as He promised, in Communion with Him. It is real. We all know it. We all share it. It is not; and it never has been the "Exclusive" property of any one group.

Again the Roman Church's "infallible" hierarchy will have to be radically restructured and the "infallibly" correct label quietly removed from some of its "Papal" dogmas. "Unity" on the principle of respecting differences and co-operating as one is, I believe the right way.

Such changes and co-operation with the rest of us - will not be a weakening but an immeasurable strengthening of the "Body of Christ."

If we are to be better equipped and happier as units "combined operations" in wisdom and love is the obvious and perhaps only way for us to go forward.

That I'm sure is the word of the "High Command" the order of the day for our future campaigning in the Christian Church now.

A dual carriageway has just been built between Aberdeen and Inverurie. It makes for easier and pleasanter travelling between them. The view of the countryside has changed and is much more interesting. Blackburn and Kintore have been by-passed, but these communities and the very many others en route are closely joined together and can move easily onto the main road and stream of journeying. Identities have not been lost. They have been enhanced. They can each function happily and effectively. Their sense of community has increased. They are all one in a new and better way. There's a lesson somewhere there.

Chapter 16

HIS NAME WAS JOHN

Do you have a favourite name? I confess, I have quite a few. For I have been lucky to have met many nice people, but out of the many I think top of the list is John. Some have had quite a significant influence in my life

John McKellar

I called him Uncle Jack but his name was John. I lived to be sorry that I had been so afraid of him. But from the first I sensed he was hurt and angry every time he saw me. And little wonder. Not long married to Alice Lister the very beautiful and lovely girl he had first seen on a holiday from his native Glasgow; he had fallen in love with her at first sight. He was an extremely clever, lively, good looking young man determined to build up a successful business in the city. Alice and he were ready to begin life together in Glasgow when it was clear things had gone wrong with her older sister Margaret. Margaret's courtship with a young farmer had stopped but she was pregnant. They decided to help her by staying on in Rothesay. Alice and Jack's dearly longed for son and Margaret's child were due about the same time. Margaret's child, myself arrived, all right. Half an hour later in the same room Alice's beautiful son was delivered still born.

For long, I had to be hidden out of sight whenever Jack came back from his long day's work in Glasgow. It took years before my Uncle and I were happy in each others company.

Fifty years after in Largo, I had celebrated the wedding of Sam Smith to Agnes Black. At the reception I sat beside the Best Man, Sam's brother, "Which part of Glasgow, do you come from?" I asked. He was broad Glasgow "I cam frae the Gorbals. I hae aye stayed there "Do you know Waddell Street? I asked. "Aye that's where a stey. I've aye stayed there!" "Did you know John McKellar of the Slaters and Plasterers?" "Aye" - his voice deepened menacingly "a real rogue yon!" "Yes" I said "that was my uncle. I used to think that too. He was really rather a nice man."

John Althorp

I was never to forget some of the officers and men of the Royal Scots Greys in the mess at Luneburg. I was a young enthusiastic but very green young Chaplain. Many of them were young too, but they had campaigned and lived as I had not. They knew that; but they welcomed me and treated me as an old friend. They gave me confidence in myself for the first time: no one more so than John Althorp. I was 26, John was 23.

He was pleasant; a courteous companion, with no side of any kind to his personality and most pleasant to be with. The first time we had anything serious to discuss, I was never to forget. I'd been told, when he went on leave, to watch for any Press photographs of Princess Elizabeth. It was known that John and the Princess were very fond of each other; and everyone was pleased about it; and genuinely hopeful that all would go well for both of them. John went on leave. I saw the reason for the "tip-off." Princess Elizabeth sported a diamond Eagle-the Grey's emblem, on her lapel; and looked very happy with it.

Part of the gratitude I have for him was the strength he gave me in my need when I was in difficulty with my superiors. In a way we were able to help each other. John's friendship with Princess Elizabeth had been broken off to his great sorrow. He confided this to me soon after. I respected his sadness and pain. For his part he was later to help me when the Army High Command rejected my wish to help Luneburg's Refugees on the order of "Non fraternisation with the Enemy." Over a whisky in the evening I had vented my anger to John. His reply "These poor people are no enemies. Fight the High Command." I did. The High Command recanted.
I never forgot John Althorp.

John Gilmour

John Gilmour was and is one of the finest men I've ever known. My wife Marion had just gone to Upper Largo in Fife in 1967. He came to the manse with his son John. They had come to welcome us to the parish. They brought a brace of pheasants with them. "We don't expect you'll have time to do any poaching yet. So we hope you'll enjoy these." I'd already heard my Session Clerk was an expert poacher so I replied "That's nice of you. I'll be busy for a wee while. Maybe Archie will give me a few tips before long. But meantime these are lovely. Thank you."

That was the beginning of a friendship with John Gilmour and his wife Ursula that my wife Marion and I found very precious indeed.

John was one of the kindest, considerate and charming men it was possible to meet. He was the owner of the Montrave Estate. He had inherited it from his father who had been Secretary of State for Scotland. Always the Gilmours had managed the Estate well and were closely associated with and respected by the community and in Largo Kirk. John was fine Elder and Conservative M.P. for North East Fife for eighteen years. I just always loved being with him and enjoyed the genuine friendship we shared. His honesty, humility and delicious sense of humour made him the popular man he deserved to be.

When he was invited by Her Majesty the Queen to be her representative at the Church of Scotland General Assembly in 1982 and 1983 all Largo was rightly happy for him. No one, I thought, and think could have had a better friend than John Gilmour.

John, my father

I had often wondered who he was and what had really happened. I'd grown up believing I had been conceived in rape.

My father and mother-in-law had retired to a house to the West of Rothesay town in Craigmore which had a splendid view of Rothesay Bay and the Kyles of Bute. One day Marion and I visited them and were introduced to two unmarried sisters next door. As we undressed for bed at night I remarked to Marion "It's very odd; but I felt a strange sort of attraction for one of these girls. I've never felt anything quite like it before." "It's not odd" replied Marion "you're sort of second cousins." I'd never discussed my family tree problems with Marion. From my teens I'd tried to put it behind me and get on with living as best I could. I never succeeded; but I didn't speak about it to anyone.

Later the next door sisters spoke to me "Your father is very ill. He'd like to see you." I went to his farm. I was met by five half brothers and sisters I didn't know of. (He had married his housekeeper after his mother died.) Two boys had the red hair I liked. All the Listers had it. I was the only odd one out. My hair was mousy brown. One of the girls, Bec, I took to very warmly. I was ushered in to the old man, my father. "Why did you never make yourself known to me?" I asked him. "I heard and saw you were a lively young boy; always getting into mischief; clever and happy" he said. "Appearances are deceptive. I was often terribly lonely and unhappy. I missed not having a father" I replied simply. "I'm sorry," he said. I didn't feel a thing for him. "I'm sorry you are ill. I hope you'll be all right" I remarked. A few pleasantries and I said "Good bye."

He died a fortnight later.

That was my father. Without whatever he was and did, I would not have existed.

John, Sandra's Brother

My last John, is perhaps the most important. I never knew of him till after I married Sandra.

I hadn't known she'd had a brother. He was the first born of the family; two years before Sandra in 1937.

He had been born horribly handicapped. His body was terribly twisted; his arms immovably stuck; his body cruelly contorted. He couldn't walk; move or do anything for himself. He could see slightly. He couldn't speak nor ever did. But he often cried terribly, heart-rendingly; painfully. It seemed endlessly; from some bottomless pit of unspeakably; but felt and surely known sorrow.

Always through life I've felt myself deeply angered by the suffering of badly handicapped people. Always I found it unjust and quite incomprehensible. That and the lives that almost are but aren't; and worse. The unseen millions; born with incurable diseases, cancers, Aids and the like, in life for days or months; in agony; then gone; never really known; forgotten as though they hadn't been; some pitiful mistake. Since my teens I always felt there had to be some kind of Heaven; if only to right the cruel injustice of the unmerited suffering of the innocent and the good.

I knew something else. How immensely indebted we are to life's disabled; earth's and physically and mentally handicapped ones and I've never been moved more by any than them. Their impairment always makes me feel more grateful and responsible for my comparative fitness than I've been. Their cheerfulness, courage and kindness, in spite of the seeming hopelessness of their condition, has often served as rebuke and encouragement,

One thing I know for sure is that John,Sandra's brother, the handicapped one I never knew or met had quite a lot to do with drawing Sandra and me together.

From our quite different backgrounds we were one in our concern for earth's suffering ones. We had learned that the Good Samaritan's response to the injured man on the dangerous Jerusalem to Jericho Road is the only right one. "He came where he was" we are told. (Luke 10:33). That way at least lies some measure of healing and hope.

The other part of the answer lay in the element of loneliness and strain of insecurity Sandra recognised in me, her Minister. We tuned in to the wavelength of need in each other.

I have little doubt that I owe Sandra to her brother,the terribly paralysed boy and brother, who speechless cried out his need for love to the world. To John McIlvride, unkown and unheard, I owe Sandra.

It is to John I owe a debt I shall never be able to repay.

Chapter 17

THE DAY I MET SANDRA

I found myself in very great pain The doctor thought that like Marion who had died nine years before; that I had some form of cancer. Then at last something was detected.

I went into Edinburgh for a suspected cancer of the aesophagus. I enjoyed the attention of James Chalmers and James Mylne anesthetists both from Aberdeen. They put me to sleep for the last operation to be performed by the brilliant Peruvian surgeon Philip Valbaum. It helps to be in the hands of dedicated and skilful surgeons who also exude the confidence drug before operations. I knew I could not be in safer or better hands.

"Which half of the stitching did you do?" I asked him when I came to. The cut had been from the right side below the waist to right under the left arm and across to the middle of the back. "My Indian colleague did half," Valbaum smiled. Two friends I'd made in the Ward, really marvellous men, died after their operations. I had again been lucky.

I had decided to retire. I was sad to have to leave a marvellous congregation in a beautiful place I moved down to a beautiful house a member of the Church had left me.

I was in some measure of trouble. One morning a letter arrived from a dear member of the congregation, Peggy Balfour. Peggy and her late husband David had been good friends of Marion and myself. In her letter Peggy quoted the last words from Euripides' Tragedy "The Alcestis."

"There be many shapes of mystery;
And many things God brings to be
Past hope or fear.
And the end men looked for cometh not,
And a path is there where no man thought.
So hath it fallen here."

What I wondered was in Peggy's mind?

I'd always enjoyed the company of fellow members of the Lundin Links Golf Club. One lovely morning there, the 20th of May 1987, over a half pint of beer I was reading "The Scotsman." I was dismayed to read the death of a good friend, Jean Scott, wife of the Rev. Leonard Scott of the West Church, Inverurie. She had been another victim of cancer. I was fond of Leonard. I knew what he, with Jean and the family, had been through. I decided, against Doctor's orders to go North and be with him. As I drove into the town, the place tugged at my heart again. The funeral over, and a visit to the Manse too, I couldn't resist the temptation to visit one or two old friends. The first was Mary Esslemont, who'd always been great fun.

"I'm dying of cancer. It won't be long" Mary said soon after I was in the door. We had ten minutes sharing and savouring what we knew would be our last meeting. After prayer, we embraced and said "Goodbye." I then visited the wife of an Elder, Jimmy Giles, who had died. Another family were not at home. From Kathy Reid's Dyce Villa, I phoned Betty Allan of Ardmurdo. Johnstone Hay was with Betty Betty had lost her husband Allan, and Johnstone's wife Betty, another beautiful Betty had just died.

I was sad, but it was like being home again I stayed the night at the Kintore Arms Hotel. At breakfast, as I read "The Press and Journal" I read that Donald McIlvride had died. In my day Donald has been in charge of the Bulb Farm, of Seymour Cobley's, Spalding Lincolnshire. I'd always loved looking at the acres and acres of fields of daffodils and tulips in the field at Port Elphinstone, Keithall and Fintray. Often I'd remembered them and Donald. He had never come to Church, but I always thought of him as a super man.

I knew I should know the family. I was annoyed with myself, that I could recall nothing more about the McIlvride family. I decided to look in to the house, for a short time, and express my sympathy before going back to Largo for a wedding rehearsal.

Quite the last thought in my mind was romance. One of my many faults, is that I hated death, and took the loss of people I loved very badly. That was exactly the state I was in As I walked down the path to the house I remember thinking of Marion Jean Scott, and now Mary Esslemont.

I opened the back gate. From the bottom of the garden came an angel smiling. "How nice to see you, Douglas" she said. It all came back as though we'd never been away from each other. "Sandra, It's nice to see you again. But I am sorry your Dad has died." I replied naturally and sincerely.

"Come in!" said Sandra. We quietly talked over exactly how things had been for both of us since Marion and I had left Inverurie.

"It's rather wonderful this, Douglas" said Sandra. "I wasn't in the least surprised, when you came through that gate. It just felt the most natural and right thing to be happening. I didn't know Mrs. Scott had died. You might have been on the moon, for all I knew. It has been so long. And now, it's as though you were still my Minister."

I felt the same way as that. I knew she would be one with me for the rest of time. "It would be nice if you came down to Largo sometime" I said as I left to go South, "I'd like that" she said.

I wrote asking her to come down, and bring her friend Helen with her.

We both knew without any slightest shadow of doubt that God had been in our meeting; that what we were feeling and wanted to do was of His, as well as our choosing.

We were married by the Rev. Phil Petty, in the presence of a few friends on June 27th 1987 in the lovely and ancient St. Monans's Church. My son David was Best Man and my daughter Alice was Bridesmaid. It was a lovely day.

The day I met Sandra, I knew I was beginning really to live for the first time. I was 66. And that is how it has been. In my marriage to Marion, I knew I had failed to be the man I wanted to be. She, being Marion, stoutly denied I had let her down in any way. She meant that, because she gave so much in every way and all the time, to and for me, the family and our congregations. She never looked for returns. She found lots to be happy about, as she gave her

Sandra, 1987

all, in all the circumstances we had known. I was far far luckier in her, than she ever was in me. I was grateful, but I still regretted failing her as I knew I did.

Without any deserving on my part, I was with Sandra. "I've loved you for thirty years" she said a few days later. "I wish you had told me ten years ago" I answered. "We have each other now, Let's make the most of every day we have" she answered happily.

97

We've both done that. Never in my wildest dreams had I ever thought of coming back to Inverurie. We'd enjoyed it once, but that was ancient history. Life moves on to "pastures new" and "new people" too.

But here we were and are again. The first time, coming to Aberdeenshire had felt like coming to a foreign land, where people spoke a strange but beautiful language, the language of Heaven, the Divine Doric.

It had taken some time for a Southern foreigner to feel at home in Inverurie. But once you settled into heaven's ways, it felt like home. And now I was back. Heaven twice, is a bit much to ask. Every day, in every street and shop, I see, walk and talk with friends of yester year, off today's "Voter's Roll" and "Electoral Register" but doubly on mine; and now I keep company and enjoy their children and grandchildren. I have a three dimensional, generational experience, and life-view every hour. This I never expected. Will Heaven be like this? I doubt if I'll ever know. Who cares? There can't be anything better than this.

There is, of course the other side of the matrimonial coin Sandra, resigned from her headship of 500 pupils and staff at Hazlehead Primary School, Aberdeen to look after me more securely.

She is beautiful, lively, highly intelligent, a great gardener, wonderful cook, and a top-class artist; a perfectionist in everything she does.

This marriage made in Heaven cannot last on earth. Still, it may perchance be born-again in Heaven.

As with Marion, marriage to Sandra is part of the pleasant union of Scotland with England. Marion's delightful dad Eddie Read and his family came from Evercreech in Somerset. Sandra's mum and dad came from Spalding in Lincolnshire. The background of two fine English families has meant much through the years.

Donald McIlvride met, courted and married Gladys in Spalding. Gladys's seven brothers had all been killed on the Battle fields of Europe in the first World War. Donald and Gladys had John; then there was Sandra. One thing I did know, I had found the loveliest girl I would ever meet. I was very, very glad.

Marion, an only and much loved child was closely attached to Church. Sandra had been in the Church and Choir during my days as Minister of St. Andrews Church. She was not naturally a Churchy person. Neither were her father and mother. Did the loss of seven brothers in the First World Ware, and a first child born incapable of being part of life, so terribly handicapped, make Church and its faith, difficult to hold with cool, assured certainty?

As with most of the vast unChurched numbers, absence from Church does not mean absence or alienation from God; or goodness, far from it.

The professionalism of family and business life, observing the highest standards in them, genuine concern for justice and mercy and a warmhearted devotion to what matters for the good of people, and charm and steadfastness in all things are surely the most truly religious of traits. Sandra, like her parents before her has been all of that.

The moment we met we knew it would be for ever. It will be.

The day I met Sandra was the happiest and quite the best day of my life. I began really to live properly for the first time that day. That is the greatest thing that can happen to any man.

With Sandra at one of her exhibitions 2003